HATRED

ALSO BY MICHAEL COREN

The Future of Catholicism (2013)

Heresy (2012)

Why Catholics Are Right (2011)

As I See It (2009)

J.R.R. Tolkien: The Man Who Created the Lord of the Rings (2001)

Setting It Right (1996)

The Man Who Created Narnia: The Story of C.S. Lewis (1994)

The Life of Sir Arthur Conan Doyle (1993)

The Invisible Man: The Life and Liberties of H.G. Wells (1993)

Aesthete (1993)

Gilbert: The Man Who Was G.K. Chesterton (1990)

The Outsiders (1985)

Theatre Royal: 100 Years of Stratford East (1985)

MICHAEL COREN

HATRED

ISLAM'S WAR ON CHRISTIANITY

SIGNAL

McCLELLAND
& STEWART

Signal is an imprint of McClelland & Stewart,
a division of Random House of Canada Limited,
a Penguin Random House Company

Library and Archives Canada Cataloguing in Publication
information available on request

ISBN: 978-0-7710-2384-2

Published simultaneously in the United States of America by
McClelland & Stewart, a division of Random House of Canada Limited
P.O. Box 1030, Plattsburgh, New York 12901

Library of Congress Control Number: 2014943617

Printed and bound in the United States of America

McClelland & Stewart,
a division of Random House of Canada Limited,
a Penguin Random House Company
www.randomhouse.ca

1 2 3 4 5   18 17 16 15 14

CONTENTS

ACKNOWLEDGEMENTS

One of the strange, paradoxical things about writing a book such as this is that it's probably a good idea not to thank and acknowledge too many people. I have already had my life threatened over what you are about to read; the first abusive letter came as soon as it was discovered that I was writing the book in the first place, warning me that there would be dire consequences if I proceeded. I chose to opt for truth rather than the alternative. So, briefly: to all of the people all over the world, and they know who they are, who gave me their time and trusted me so deeply, thank you from the bottom of my heart. To my family, to my publishers, to my editors, and to my colleagues I am, as always, immensely grateful. I dedicate this book to those followers of Christ who live a daily life of dignity and faith in the midst of degradation and danger. Religious persecution, any religious persecution, is always repugnant but the experience of so many Christians is made all the worse because so few people seem to know about it, and when they do know seem to prefer not to care. An open, bleeding wound in the international body politic. I hope and pray that in the most authentic sense this book can acknowledge the new persecuted.

HATRED

INTRODUCTION

IN THE SUMMER OF 2012 I interviewed an evangelical minister and activist on my nightly television current affairs show in Canada. I've hosted this program, *The Arena*, on the Sun News Network for almost four years now, having hosted and produced a former show of a similar style on another network for thirteen years. On both of them I have tried to discuss, among numerous and various other issues, the international persecution of Christians, especially within Islam; I do this because, tragically and regrettably, there is never a shortage of newsworthy and timely opportunities to do so and also because so few other broadcasters and journalists are prepared to devote sufficient time to this acutely pertinent and important subject. They seem to prefer the banal to the biting, the easy to the essential. On this occasion my guest, who had vast experience of the horrors faced by followers of Christ in Muslim majority states in particular, asked me if he could put a Bible on the desk in front of him during the interview. Always reluctant to resemble a Christian television show – I am not criticizing what they do, but it is simply not my mandate and does tend to exclude many potential audience members – I politely told him that I'd rather he didn't. Gracious and understanding, he said he fully appreciated my response. But, he continued, this particular Bible might be of interest to the viewers and to me as he had been given it by an Iraqi Christian who was a parishioner at Our Lady of Salvation Syriac Catholic cathedral in Baghdad

1

and had been present at the church during the evening mass on October 31, 2010. I knew immediately to what he was referring. That was the date when a Sunni Muslim terrorist group known as the Islamic State of Iraq launched a concerted attack on the church, murdering at least fifty-eight people and wounding more than seventy-five.

The large heavy book being held in front of me was, I realized, almost beyond reading. Its pages were thick, curled, and glued together in purple lumps, soaked in and sticky with the blood of the men, women, and children who had been slaughtered that warm evening in a place of peace, in a city where Christians had lived and flourished before Islam even existed. This was not a holy book to be preached from, but a holy book of martyrdom that preached. Its hardly legible pages spoke entire volumes, its red-turned-to-brown stains cried out to a still largely indifferent or even hostile world. I felt guilty that day, ashamed, judgmental, and rather small. The Bible stayed on the desk, the interview took place, and I have seldom in four thousand episodes of television been as moved as I was by that encounter. At the end of the interview, the minister showed me some of the shell casings and shrapnel that he had picked up from the floor of the church, the grotesque detritus of the pogrom that took place that night. I asked him if I could keep some of them, and he agreed. I have them still, and they are in front of me right now as I write these words. Every few paragraphs I stop, pick them up, and roll them in my hands as if they were a relic or rosary beads: a tactile reminder, a startling flashback to a scene whose agony I can only imagine. It is one of the reasons, but only one, that I feel duty bound to write this book.

The Baghdad attack, however, was merely one example of the Islamic war on Christianity that has been under way for so very long. An exhaustive list of the individual and collective acts of terror, violence, abuse, and militant discrimination is almost impossible, but I will in this book detail many of the most repugnant of them, and other acts and actions that reveal the routine, grinding nature of daily life for Christians in the Islamic heartlands. Some of the lists I present in the following chapters may be difficult to read, so repetitive in their horror that they become numbing. But they have to be written, because without doing so I cannot present the authentic reality of Christian life in the Muslim world, and also because so few people have any idea of just how bloody that reality has become.

But before we proceed, we also need to establish two foundational aspects of this subject. First, it is surely obvious and self-evident that not all Muslims behave in such an intolerant and violent way and that hundreds of millions of them are appalled by what is going on. More than this, moderate, progressive, and secular Muslims are often victims of Islamic radicalism just as are Christians. It's also true that Islam itself has not always been as anti-Christian and triumphalist as it is at this point in its history, but then again it would be facile and misleading to assume that the religion itself embraces theological equality and egalitarian social co-existence. It might be comforting to assume that intolerance is an aberration within Islam but, as we will see later, discrimination against Christians or any other non-Muslims is in fact integral to orthodox Muslim teaching, and the more profound issue to the serious-minded is not the existence of sectarianism but its extent.

The second point to make is that persecution of Christians is not confined to Islam. North Korea, for example, arrests, tortures, and executes Christian worshippers and leaders to an appalling degree, and Islam, obviously, has nothing to do with it. But North Korea is a rancid and psychotic post-Communist dictatorship governed by paranoia and lies. It persecutes any group or person likely to challenge the regime, is not genuinely ideological, does not seek to export Christian persecution, and has no long-term future. Communist China also persecutes Christians, allowing officially sanctioned churches but monitoring and harassing those who will not submit to central control. Once again, though, the Chinese do this not because they want to destroy Christianity but because they are obsessed with unanimity. It doesn't diminish the horror of the persecution but it does put it in a different context from the Islamic horror. The Chinese government's attitude toward Christians is, quite simply, radically different from that of most Islamic governments and societies. Being a Christian in China is not the same as being one in, for example, Pakistan, Iraq, or Sudan.

Then there is India, where Christianity has thrived for two thousand years. Indian Christianity is said to have begun with the arrival of St. Thomas, it certainly expanded with the arrival of the Portuguese more than fourteen hundred years later, and it was solidified by both French and British conquest. Yet there have been grotesque massacres of Christians in parts of India, inspired by Hindu nationalist mobs. Because of the enormous population of India, the numbers of people injured and killed is horrible, and it's vital that this isn't downplayed. But what must be emphasized is that this is entirely atypical of Indian society and attitudes, that the Indian authorities abhor this and prosecute and punish those involved, that India is a genuinely pluralistic society, and that Indian Christians do not live in fear and submission the way that Christians even in neighbouring Pakistan do. Indeed, in a chapter on Pakistan I will discuss the blasphemy laws, the mass violence, and the persecution of Christians in that Islamic state. No Indian Christian living in the diaspora is nervous of going back to India for a vacation or a visit – my mother-in-law is one such – while Pakistani Christians keep in regular contact with their relatives back home in Pakistan to make sure that they have survived the week.

Islamic persecution, on the other hand, is not dominated or even shaped by local circumstances, political context, racial tensions, or historic relationships. One of its most shocking qualities is its universality: Africans in Nigeria and Somalia, Arabs in Egypt and Syria, Asians in Malaysia and Indonesia, Turks in Turkey, Persians in Iran, and so on. The overriding and defining reason is the religion of the persecutor and the religion of the persecuted. And Islam, in its most conservative form, is expanding. While communism is moribund, Islamic fundamentalism is the very opposite. The persecution of Christians in the non-Muslim world is, I believe, not a long-term problem and is, anyway, written about elsewhere. Islam's war on Christianity is expanding all the time and is far too seldom even mentioned. There are, however, cracks developing in the opaque window of denial.

In February 2014, U.S. representative Chris Smith, chairman of the congressional panel that oversees international human rights issues, told a congressional subcommittee that discussion of "anti-Christian persecution is not meant to minimize the suffering of other religious minorities who are imprisoned or killed for their beliefs" but to make it clear that Christians "remain the most persecuted religious group the world over."[1] But he could and should have gone further. Anthony Browne is the Europe correspondent of *The Times* and, as he says himself, is a "godless atheist whose soul doesn't want to be saved, thank you." As such, what he wrote about Christian persecution is all the more poignant.

After outlining how more than 300 million Christians are threatened with violence or face legal discrimination, forced conversion, and daily threats, Browne wrote of Saudi Arabia, where churches, public Christian worship, and the Bible are banned, and non-Muslims are prevented from entering Mecca and even becoming citizens, and when they do live in the country are frequently imprisoned and tortured on false charges of drinking and blasphemy.

"The Copts of Egypt," he continued, "make up half the Christians in the Middle East, the cradle of Christianity. They inhabited the land before the Islamic conquest, and still make up a fifth of the population. By law they are banned from being president of the Islamic Republic of Egypt or attending Al Azhar University, and severely restricted from joining the police and army. By practice they are banned from holding any high political or commercial position. Under the 19th-century Hamayouni decrees, Copts must get permission from the president to build or repair churches – but he usually refuses. Mosques face no such controls. Government-controlled TV broadcasts anti-Copt propaganda, while giving no airtime to Copts. It is illegal for Muslims to convert to Christianity, but legal for Christians to convert to Islam. Christian girls – and even the wives of Christian priests – are abducted and forcibly converted to Islam.

"In the Islamic Republic of Pakistan, most of the five million Christians live as an underclass, doing work such as toilet cleaning. Under the Hudood ordinances, a Muslim can testify against a non-Muslim in court, but a non-Muslim cannot testify against a Muslim. Blasphemy laws are abused to persecute

Christians. In the last few years, dozens of Christians have been killed in bomb and gun attacks on churches and Christian schools. In Nigeria, 12 states have introduced Sharia law, which affects Christians as much as Muslims. Christian girls are forced to wear the Islamic veil at school, and Christians are banned from drinking alcohol. Thousands of Christians have been killed in the last few years in the ensuing violence."

None of this is news to those who have followed the lives of Christians in the Islamic world, but Browne is sufficiently honest and perceptive to explain why so little has been done to deal with this issue and to speak clearly and honestly. "The trouble is that the trendies who normally champion human rights seem to think persecution is fine, so long as it's only against Christians. While Muslims openly help other Muslims, Christians helping Christians has become as taboo as jingoistic nationalism. . . . Part of the problem is old-style racism against non-whites; part of it is new-style guilt. If all this were happening to the world's Sikhs or Muslims simply because of their faith, you can be sure it would lead the *10 O'Clock News* and the front page of the *Guardian* on a regular basis. As a liberal democrat atheist, I believe all persecuted people should be helped equally, irrespective of their religion. But the guilt-ridden West is ignoring people because of their religion."[2]

Quite so. The persecution itself is repugnant but the largely indifferent response from those with power and influence makes it all the worse. Christian leaders from countries where their flocks are persecuted look to the Western world for help and expect that those who routinely speak out for and about all sorts of human rights – some of them rather tenuous – will respond and help them. Their trust is touching but in a way pathetic. Christians simply do not fit the description of what so many in Europe and North America regard as a persecuted class. This cultivated apathy is made all the easier because so many significant and wealthy countries, politicians, and leaders identify themselves as Christians, and I am sure many of them are. The United States in particular is a self-identified Christian nation, and its Republican presidents in particular have made a point of declaring their Christian faith. They haven't, though, done very much to help their brethren and, in the case of the war on Iraq, have made their situation far worse. But because these leaders are known as Christians it makes it all the easier for those who are not and who do not care about the Christian plight under Islam to dismiss the idea of Christian suffering as being absurd. Christians are the ones with the power, they argue, and they are more the oppressors than the oppressed. It's a banal, suburban, unworldly, and naïve response but it also enables almost unimaginable human suffering.

There is also the phenomenon of the racism of lowered expectations. White liberals, while aghast when accused, almost seem to expect Muslim leaders and cultures to behave differently and worse than Western and Christian or post-Christian leaders and cultures. It's one of the reasons that Israel is always held to a far higher ethical standard than its neighbours. "The Jews are more like us but the Arabs are not" runs the cry. It's sinister and patronizing, but those of us who have seen it at first-hand have no doubts. Apart from the inherent foolishness of this approach, it fails to take into account the fact that Christians in the Islamic world are also Arabs or African or Asian and that in some of those countries it is they and not the Islamic majority who form the underclass. It would be encouraging, even liberating, to explain that at least Western Christians who take their faith seriously are aware of the situation and are fighting back. In some cases that's true, but for the most part it's not, and not enough, and sometimes almost nothing is being done. Evangelical churches are occasionally active, Anglican leaders have made helpful statements, the Eastern Orthodox churches – with many adherents in the Arab Muslim world – have frequently protested persecution and violence, and the Vatican is obviously in touch with daily events, but truth be told this is all too little.

In the 2013 apostolic exhortation *Evangelii Gaudium*, Pope Francis wrote: "I ask and I humbly entreat those countries to grant Christians freedom to worship and to practice their faith, in light of the freedom which followers of Islam enjoy in Western countries! Faced with disconcerting episodes of violent fundamentalism, our respect for true followers of Islam should lead us to avoid hateful generalizations, for authentic Islam and the proper reading of the Koran are opposed to every form of violence." His call for Christian freedom is noble but many would argue that his statement that authentic Koranic and Islamic teaching prohibits violence is optimistic to the point of absurdity or even irresponsibility; the precise persecution Christians face is justified and explained by Muslims by their holy book and the teachings of their faith, and while it may be one interpretation of the Koran it is one that appears to dominate the Islamic-Christian relationship and narrative. With all due respect, one has to wonder how much experience a man from Argentina now living in Rome has of the daily lives of Christians living in the Muslim world, especially if he is being advised by people who might perhaps have their own perspectives and, dare we say, agendas.

There are, of course, courageous and forthright voices, and some of them are Muslim. In November 2013, the British

Conservative politician Lady Warsi, a long-term campaigner against extremism within her own Muslim faith, made a speech at Georgetown University in Washington D.C. She warned of the extinction of Christianity in the Middle East, with an exodus of a "Biblical scale" taking place. This came after repeated attacks on Christians in Syria and Egypt, but also outside of the Arab region in Pakistan; in Peshawar two months earlier eighty-five Christians had been massacred. Warsi wrote in Britain's *Daily Telegraph* that "there are parts of the world today where to be a Christian is to put your life in danger. From continent to continent, Christians are facing discrimination, ostracism, torture, even murder, simply for the faith they follow. Christian populations are plummeting and the religion is being driven out of some of its historic heartlands. In Iraq, the Christian community has fallen from 1.2 million in 1990 to 200,000 today. In Syria, the horrific bloodshed has masked the hemorrhaging of its Christian population."[3]

Shortly before Christmas 2013, Prince Charles spoke out about Islamic extremism and its persecution of Christians. This was unusual and important because the royal family seldom discusses such issues and because the Prince of Wales has always been regarded as a trusted friend of the Muslim community in Britain and abroad. "It seems to me," he said, "that we cannot ignore the fact that Christians in the Middle East are, increasingly, being deliberately attacked by fundamentalist Islamist militants. Christianity was, literally, born in the Middle East and we must not forget our Middle Eastern brothers and sisters in Christ. For 20 years, I have tried to build bridges between Islam and Christianity and to dispel ignorance and misunderstanding. The point though, surely, is that we have now reached a crisis where the bridges are rapidly being deliberately destroyed by those with a vested interest in doing so, and this is achieved through intimidation, false accusation and organized persecution, including to Christian communities in the Middle East at the present time."[4]

Father Zakaria Boutros is a Coptic Orthodox priest and a gentle, thoughtful man. He is one of the leading figures of the Egyptian Coptic Christian community but is now obliged to live in exile in the United States after twice being arrested in his homeland; Muslims in Iran and Saudi Arabia have put a $60-million bounty on his head. While he is anonymous to most North Americans and Europeans, Boutros is famous – or notorious – throughout North Africa, the Middle East, and Central Asia, where his daily television broadcasts attract enormous audiences and his website millions of hits. His style is uncompromising. Speaking in Egyptian-accented Arabic and fluent in Islamic scholarship and the various subcultures of the Muslim world, he carefully unwraps the layers of the Koran and the life and teachings of Mohammad and presents his viewers with a virtually unprecedented critique of their faith. It's the combination of accessibility and originality that makes him so threatening to militant Islam. "Look, we know people are leaving Islam because of what I say and the Muslims know people are leaving Islam because of what I say," he explains. A long pause, then: "People in the West simply don't understand the significance of this in a Muslim world that has not and probably will not embrace pluralism. The Islamic response is not to argue with me but to try to kill me. But leaving aside my attempts to convert people, which is my right, there is the persecution of Christians throughout the Muslim world who are not trying to convert people at all but merely trying to live their lives as Christians and not hurt anyone. They don't have to be religious, devout, or active Christians to be persecuted – just be Christians. [They are] persecuted for being what they are."

Persecuted for being what they are. It epitomizes the situation. Encounters with people such as Father Boutros and with legions of people – men and women, black and white, old and young – who have lived as Christians in the Muslim world and who have told me their stories and shared their pain have made this more than a political or professional issue. It is personal. I wish I could convey their fear and brokenness in the way they deserve and express the depth of injustice and suffering that exists. Frankly, I doubt that I can. What I am not attempting to do in this book is to provide a full and extensive history of Islam and of Christianity, of the relationship between the two, or to give a full analysis of Islam's persecution of Christianity and Christians. That would require a very different and much longer book. What I am trying to do is to show the reality of the situation, to outline how this phenomenon is not about religion in general but Islam in particular, how the world has to respond and deal with the situation, and why we cannot, must not, hide behind politically correct clichés and sheer cowardice. Let us be candid. People are reluctant to criticize Islam because they are frightened of being accused of racism or what is absurdly known as Islamophobia, because they are nervous of being associated with Christianity or some canard of a conservative agenda, and because they are terrified of physical violence. There are, as we know, numerous examples of Western critics or even apolitical cartoonists and writers who have been threatened with death and in some cases have been murdered by Islamic radicals. I myself have been threatened and, as I said earlier, was even warned not to write this book. None of these are arguments for silence but mere excuses, and shameful ones at that. It is not the first time that those who should have spoken loudly and forcefully against persecution have preferred to say nothing. Have we not learned from the tragic, terrible mistakes of the past?

I have structured the book in such a way as to provide a context to Islam's approach and hostility toward Christianity, explaining some of the theology and history of the relevant beliefs and relationships. I have chosen various parts of the Muslim world to write about to try to provide an overall picture that reflects different cultures, races, and regions – the notion that Islamic hatred toward Christianity is purely a geographical or politically local phenomenon is simply untrue. For this reason, I have included a chapter on Syria and Iraq (juxtaposed because the Christian experience has been fairly similar); Egypt, at the heartland of the Arab world; Iran – which is Persian and not Arab and where persecution is of a different nature; Pakistan, which is not Arab and not of the Middle East and specifically south Asian; Indonesia, separate from all the above in its history and a country founded on pluralism; Nigeria, obviously different again and composed of both Muslim and Christian populations and part of a continent that contains numerous cultures, tribes, and faiths; and a collection of other countries dealt with more briefly, including Turkey, Saudi Arabia, and Mali. The list is, tragically, far from extensive. The book ends with an analysis of what the future might hold.

This brief volume is an attempt to speak truth to Islamic power, and to explain that Christians are treated so appallingly under Islam not because of accident but by design. It is an attempt to cut through the usual and tired responses that there are reasonable explanations as to what is happening and even

– and I have heard many – justifications and valid and understandable reasons for the situation. It is an attempt to scream to
the world that it is far too late to say nothing; it has been for
some time. Pray God that people will listen.

THE CONTEXT

BEFORE WE LOOK AT how Islam and many of its followers treat Christians in the Islamic world, we need to ask some basic and essential questions about the actual teachings of the Muslim faith. What do Islam and the Koran teach about Christians? Are some Muslims betraying their religion by being intolerant and violent toward Christians – or the very opposite? And is this phenomenon not about Islam at all but a result of history, geopolitics, and various nationalist liberation struggles? The first place to turn is obviously the Koran itself, because that is where Muslims turn. We also need to quote it at some length, both to respect its integrity and to show what it actually says rather than give a single or biased impression. There is a great deal of obfuscation, confusion, and even propaganda surrounding the issue of what the Koran says. Non-Muslims are often told that they do not understand the Koran. They are told this even by Muslims – the vast majority within the Islamic world – who do not speak or read Arabic, the language of the Koran. Many Arabs who are raised with the Arabic language do not read it; Egypt, for example, is more than a quarter illiterate and Syria more than 20 percent; non-Arabic-speaking but Islamic Pakistan is more than 40 percent illiterate, and Afghanistan more than 70 percent! So there are millions of Muslims who allow others to read and interpret their holy book for them. This leads to myriad problems and dangers.

In the Koran itself, Christians are generally referred to as "people of the book" and in the various suras and ayahs, or chapters and verses, a number of other references are made. In 2:120, "Never will the Jews nor the Christians be pleased with you till you follow their religion. Say: 'Verily, Islamic Guidance is the only Guidance.' And if you were to follow their desires after what you have received of Knowledge, then you would have against Allah neither any protector nor helper." In 3:56: "As to those who disbelieve, I will punish them with a severe torment in this world and in the Hereafter, and they will have no helpers." In 3:85: "And whoever seeks a religion other than Islam, it will never be accepted of him, and in the Hereafter he will be one of the losers." In 3:118: "O you who believe! Take not as your helpers or friends those outside your religion since they will not fail to do their best to corrupt you. They desire to harm you severely. Hatred has already appeared from their mouths, but what their breasts conceal is far worse. Indeed we have made plain to you the verses if you understand." 3:178 has: "And let not the disbelievers think that our postponing of their punishment is good for them. We postpone the punishment only so that they may increase in sinfulness. And for them is a disgracing torment." Hardly encouraging or the basis for a peaceful co-existence and a comfortable pluralism.[1]

Sometimes the Koran changes emphasis or flavour, but it must be remembered – and this is vital – that the parts of the book written later supersede and abrogate those composed earlier, not necessarily those that come later in the Koran itself but those written earlier even if listed later in Islam's holy book. This means that the Koran can be quoted to appear more liberal and progressive than it is intended to be. With regard to Christianity, however, the approach seems to remain static and constant. In 5:14: "And from those who call themselves Christians, we took their covenant, but they have abandoned a good part of the Message that was sent to them. So we planted amongst them enmity and hatred till the Day of Resurrection, and Allah will inform them of what they used to do." Soon after, 5:51 has: "O you who believe! Take not the Jews and the Christians as friends, they are but friends to one another. And if any amongst you takes them as friends, then surely he is one of them. Verily, Allah guides not those people who are the wrongdoers," and in 5:73: "Surely, disbelievers are those who said: 'Allah is the third of the three (in a Trinity).' But there is no god but Allah. And if they cease not from what they say, verily, a painful torment will befall the disbelievers among them."[2]

Matters don't improve for Christians, and as we move forward we have 8:39 that says: "And fight them until there is no more disbelief in Islam and the religion will all be for Allah Alone. . . ." and in 9:23: "O you who believe! Take not for supporters your fathers and your brothers if they prefer disbelief to Belief. And whoever of you does so, then he is one of the wrongdoers." Then 9:29 says: "Fight against those who (1) believe not in Allah, (2) nor in the Last Day, (3) nor forbid that which has been forbidden by Allah and His Messenger (4) and those who acknowledge not Islam as the religion of truth among the people of the Scripture, until they pay the Jizyah [religious tax] with willing submission, and feel themselves subdued"; 9:30 states: "And those Jews (who came to you) say (as did some Jews who lived before): 'Ezra ('Uzayr) is God's son'; and (as a general assertion) the Christians say: 'The Messiah is God's son.' Such are merely their verbal assertions in imitation of the utterances of some unbelievers who preceded them. May God destroy them! How can they be turned away from the truth and make such assertions?" Next, 9:34 tells Muslims: "O you who believe! Verily, there are many of the Jewish rabbis and the Christian monks who devour the wealth of mankind in falsehood, and hinder men from the Way of Allah. And those who hoard up gold and silver, and spend it not in the Way of Allah – announce unto them a painful torment." Finally, 9:123: "O you who believe! Fight those of the disbelievers who are close to you, and let them find harshness in you, and know that Allah is with those who are the pious."[3]

It's an intolerant, aggressive language that calls directly for violence and oppression by Muslims against Christians. The common, usual reaction to these references by Muslim apologists is to argue that the Bible also calls for violence and intolerance, but this is not quite the case. The truth is that while there are certainly descriptions of violence in Christian scripture – the crucifixion is hardly a gentle scene – there are no direct calls for violence. In the New Testament, the founder of Christianity, Jesus Christ, is a man of ultimate and supreme peace who reprimands His followers when they consider, or in one case, commit violence; when Jesus is arrested in the Garden of Gethsemane, Simon Peter draws a sword and slashes off the right ear of Malchus, the servant of the high priest. Jesus condemns the action and heals the man, even though He knows the result of the arrest will be His own execution. Christ demands from those who will accept Him an unbounded mercy, a total forgiveness, a complete gentleness, and a commitment to turning the other cheek and loving one's enemy. He does on one occasion tell His followers to carry a weapon when they walk the roads in case they are attacked, and He does at the Jerusalem Temple overturn the tables of men selling bruised animals for sacrifice to God, but this is largely symbolic and, anyway, never directly violent. Indeed, many Christians have embraced complete pacifism due to their faith in Jesus and their reading of the New Testament.

The Old Testament certainly describes acts of war and violence and at specific times in its history of the Jewish people depicts God calling on His people to fight a war or organize violent resistance, even to the harshest of degrees. Christians, however, believe that the Old Testament can be understood only through the prism of the New. It just might be the reason why we see so few Lutheran suicide bombers or Methodists calling for holy war against those who do not embrace Protestantism! Of course, crimes and violence have been committed by Christians and sometimes in the name of their religion, but then crimes and violence are committed in the name of love, freedom, and democracy. The point is that any Christian who hurts another is doing so in spite of and not because of the teachings of Christ. Religions simply do not teach the same things any more than political ideas teach the same things and such a claim is an insult to religion and to common sense.

Unlike the founder of Christianity, the founder of Islam – Mohammad – was not a man of peace but at least in part a warlord. He spent the final decade of his life, from 622 to 632, as the leader of Medina and in command of its war with the then pagan city of Mecca. He and his men attacked other tribes and communities, raided caravans, and eventually triumphed in armed conflict. Often these battles and raids were carried out, it has to be said, in response to provocation, and warfare was of course by no means unique in seventh-century society among all religions and cultures. But in all this Mohammad was clearly a radically different person from Jesus. But surely

Christians have fought wars in the name of their faith, runs the counter. They certainly have, usually long ago and far less frequently than the modern world would have us believe. Also, to assume that conflicts such as those in Northern Ireland or the Balkans are purely religious is to misunderstand the nature of ethnicity and politics: these were not Catholics fighting Protestants for religious domination or Catholics fighting Orthodox Christians for theological control but contemporary tribes fighting geopolitical battles rooted in land, family, and power. Once again, Christians behave violently in spite and not because of the teachings of Jesus Christ. The same cannot be said of Muslims and the Koran.[4]

Another component of the Islamic attitude toward Christians living among them is what the author Bat Ye'or described in a word she coined in 1983. The word is *dhimmitude*, taken from the Muslim concept of the *dhimmi*. The word means "protected" in Arabic and was given historically, and is still applied, to non-Muslims conquered by Islam. It's something of a euphemism at best, and seldom did the Christians living as *dhimmi* enjoy genuine protection. "Dhimmitude is the direct consequence of jihad," writes Ye'or. "It embodie[s] all the Islamic laws and customs applied over a millennium on the vanquished population, Jews and Christians, living in the countries conquered by jihad and therefore Islamized. [We can observe a] return of the jihad ideology since the 1960s, and of some dhimmitude practices in Muslim countries applying the sharia [Islamic] law, or inspired by it. I stress . . . the incompatibility between the concept of tolerance as expressed by the jihad-dhimmitude ideology, and the concept of human rights based on the equality of all human beings and the inalienability of their rights."[5]

The history of the relationship between Muslims and Christians and the place of the *dhimmi* reveals a great deal about the modern situation. Mohammed himself wrote that if the non-believer would embrace Islam "you will be safe," and since much of Arabia in the seventh century was part of the Byzantine Empire and Christian this meant that the prophet was generally speaking to followers of Christ when he made this offer. Persia, as opposed to Arabia, was not part of a Christian empire but many of its inhabitants were nevertheless Christian. So from the period of the Islamic conquest onwards millions of Christians were obliged to live under Islamic rule, and their options were to convert to the Muslim faith, to risk death by disobeying Islamic teachings, or to pay a heavy poll tax so as to be permitted, when fortunate, to live in relative safety but in subjugation.

The place and experience of the *dhimmi* changed, of course, according to the culture of the rulers and the climate of the era. In pure definition, the relationship between Muslim and *dhimmi* was always one of relative humiliation but not necessarily, it has to be said, of downright persecution. For example, Christians were not allowed to ride horses because this could make them higher than a Muslim, so even if they were wealthy, they were obliged to ride a mule or donkey and thus appear to be slow, humble, almost childlike. They could not carry swords, making them vulnerable and weak and rather unmanly according to the customs of the time, and they were forbidden to build new churches or repair old and decaying ones unless they were given specific permission, which was usually withheld. They were not allowed to proclaim their faith publicly and if accused of so doing – sometimes falsely due to personal vendettas or disagreements – could face harsh financial and physical punishment. They were certainly not allowed to try to convert a Muslim to Christianity and would be executed if found to have done so or even attempted to have done so. Christians, as *dhimmis*, were not permitted to distribute their holy books in public places or read them to non-Christians, crosses were not allowed even in private homes or in churches, and Christians as well as Jews often had to wear types of clothes or badges that distinguished them from Muslims and made them clearly identifiable – a lesson learned by future generations of oppressors, Muslim and non-Muslim alike.

No Christian, or *dhimmi*, was allowed to testify in any court of law against a Muslim because the word of a Christian was considered unreliable if it contradicted that of a Muslim, and while Muslim men could marry Christian women, a Christian man was forbidden from marrying a Muslim woman – the assumption being that a wife would eventually convert to her husband's faith. The children of these inter-religious unions had always to be raised as Muslims. If a Christian woman married to a Christian man became a Muslim, she was given custody of their children and was permitted to divorce her husband, and in some Muslim societies the law of sharia and *dhimmis* allowed a Muslim husband to prevent his Christian wife from attending church and even gave him the right to physically incarcerate his wife at home so as to stop her worshipping with other Christians.

That the word *dhimmi* actually means, with no sense of irony, "free" or people living under a "treaty of protection" is especially absurd when we consider that these conquered people who were at best tolerated had to pay a special tax, a *jizya*, for this degrading "protection" and to live obediently under the laws of sharia. Co-existence obviously did occur, otherwise there would be no Christians left in the Islamic world. But at its most enlightened understanding and interpretation, the application of the *dhimmi* concept created a timid if relatively secure, subservient if financially successful underclass of Christians living in societies they had usually built in the first place. When, however, the status of *dhimmi* was understood and applied in a less enlightened manner, it led to persecution, abuse, and a rigid two-tier society that led inevitably to mass exile, conversion, and suffering. It was a recipe for ethnic cleansing.

Another term that is regularly used and directly pertinent to the contemporary relationship between Muslim and Christian is that of jihad, which is generally translated as "holy war" but more accurately means "to struggle" or "to strive." The defence of jihad rests on its interpretation as a form of inner struggle or cleansing, or an individual Muslim's internal battle against sin. If that were the only interpretation, it would be entirely laudable and little different from Christian and other religious notions of self-analysis and catharsis. For many Muslims there is certainly some truth in this. But there is equal if not greater truth in the definition of jihad as an external, armed struggle, a holy war, against the infidel, the unbeliever, and, most frequently, the Christian. As we saw in the various Koranic passages and verses quoted above, there is much in Islam that would lead to the latter interpretation and lead Muslims to conduct war against unbelievers. While the Hanafi, Malaki, and Hanbali schools of Islamic thought do indeed argue that jihad should be purely and exclusively undertaken in self-defence, they and certainly many of their followers expand the idea of self-defence to include attacks on any who might in the future attack Islam or who they regard as having attacked Islam, a belief that can include pretty much anyone. The Shafi'i school of jurisprudence doesn't even make the argument for jihad as self-defence and encourages all-out aggressive pre-emptive strikes on opponents of Islam and enemies of Muslims. There are various centres of authorities within Islam but no central, overriding teaching office, magisterium, or papacy as within Roman Catholicism, so behaviour is left to the individual Muslim and that individual's understanding of the Koran; having said this, nor is there any central authority in Judaism or the various Protestant churches, but Judaism and Protestantism have never produced advocates of holy war in such consistent numbers over so many extended periods of time. Jihad means holy war, and holy war to countless Muslims means armed struggle against those who do not accept and embrace Islam.[6]

This was seen clearly as the Ottoman Empire extended its power and as more Christians were ruled by Muslims and by Islam. As more campaign jihads were conducted and were victorious, more Christians were conquered and more *dhimmis* were created. Ottoman Turkey was a dominant empire, threatening its neighbours and always expansionist. During the nineteenth century, however, Turkish and thus Islamic power declined and Britain and France in particular had more sway over the Ottoman Empire – both countries were allied to it and came to its rescue during the Crimean War. As a result, the lives of Christians improved slightly, partly to improve the reputation of Turkey with its partners but also due to the direct pressure of those partners. But there were still massacres of Christians, and during the First World War the grotesque attempted genocide of Armenian Christians by the Turks took place, killing more than 1.5 million Armenian men, women, and children. This will be discussed at greater length in the penultimate chapter of the book.

When it comes to *dhimmis*, the official status of Christians in the contemporary world may not be as formally subservient as it once was, but Christians are still legally at a massive disadvantage and in practical terms never enjoy anything even approaching equality. The idea of the *dhimmi* also permeates the Islamic psyche and has led to an assumption, an accepted self-evident truth, that the Christian is seldom if ever to be completely trusted or treated on the same level as a Muslim. This attitude doesn't always manifest itself in every Muslim society and sometimes leads to only mild discrimination, but increasingly in the past thirty years it has led to wholesale persecution and endemic violence. As we will see later, at its worst it produces organized campaigns to make entire regions and countries Christian-free, to be achieved by killing, conversion, or exile.

One of the central planks in the relationship between Muslims and Christians is the so-called Pact of Umar, allegedly signed by the second caliph, Umar I (634–44). We don't know all the details of the treaty or even its precise date, and some historians argue that it was written by the conquered Christians themselves. We do know that it is used, or exploited, by modern Islamic scholars to underpin their attitudes toward Christian minorities. Among its conditions are the following:

"We shall not build, in our cities or in their neighborhood, new monasteries, churches, convents, or monks' cells, nor shall we repair, by day or by night, such of them as fall in ruins or are situated in the quarters of the Muslims. We shall keep our gates wide open for passersby and travelers. We shall give board and lodging to all Muslims who pass our way for three days. We shall not manifest our religion publicly nor convert anyone to it. We shall not prevent any of our kin from entering Islam if they wish it. We shall show respect toward the Muslims, and we shall rise from our seats when they wish to sit. We shall not seek to resemble the Muslims by imitating any of their garments, the cap, the turban, footwear, or the parting of the hair. We shall not speak as they do, nor shall we adopt their surnames. We shall not mount on saddles, nor shall we gird swords nor bear any kind of arms nor carry them on our persons.

"We shall not sell fermented drinks. We shall shave the fronts of our heads. We shall not display our crosses or our books in the roads or markets of the Muslims. We shall use only clappers [wooden noisemakers used to call people to worship] in our churches very softly. We shall not raise our voices when following our dead. We shall not carry lighted candles on any of the roads of the Muslims or in their markets. We shall not bury our dead near the Muslims."

Whatever its accuracy, chronology, and origin, it has been employed by Islam for fifteen hundred years to subjugate Christians. But surely, some contend, even if it's completely authentic, the pact was merely an example of the ugliness of medieval and pre-Enlightenment religion and society, and minorities were treated badly in many societies of the past, whatever their religiosity. There is some but limited truth in that argument, but even if we take it at face value, most Christian countries did certainly change their attitude toward religious minorities, with western Europe and the United States leading the way. The aberration of German Nazism was pagan rather than Christian and was in fact a direct response to the love and gentleness of the New Testament. Any genuine reading of National Socialist ideologues makes this entirely obvious. Tragically, many modern critics of Christianity prefer Internet sound bites to genuine scholarship. Remember, there is no separation of mosque and state in Islamic thought, no possibility of granting full and absolute equality in any Muslim state to those who are not members of the mosque.

Which bring us to the Crusades, which are used by defenders of Islam and those who try to forgive Islamic persecution of Christians to explain why Muslims feel and act the way they do. No matter how badly Christians may have been treated by Muslims, runs the defence, the Christians behaved worse during the Crusades and this episode of naked aggression and imperialism shaped Muslim responses to Christians for the rest of time. Well, not quite, not quite by a very long way. The story runs as follows: long, long ago in a country far, far away, armies of brutish, greedy, and stupid men with crosses on their chests invaded a peaceful and tolerant land and tried to convert people to Christianity; when, that is, they were not slaughtering innocent boys and girls or refusing to learn to read and write or, perish the thought, take a simple bath once in a while. Thus the Crusades. Christians bad, Muslims good. It tends to be the first attack we hear because of a whole club of issues: the rise of Islamic radicalism, the crisis in the Middle East, and the fact that Muslim extremists who know even less about history than Western anti-Christians label everyone who isn't Muslim and who lives in Europe and North America as Crusaders. It's also horribly relevant to today's Muslim persecution of Christians.

It's presented in mass-market fiction, in much of even credible media, and in many lecture halls and classrooms. This was the time when the Pope revealed Christianity to be truly animalistic and violent. It was pre-Reformation of course, so Protestants manage to avoid the nonsense. It was that great moral theologian and medieval historian Kevin Costner in the movie *Robin Hood, Prince of Thieves* who explained that his father, Robin Hood senior, was opposed to the Crusades because he thought it foolish and wrong to try to convert others to your own religion. Robin and his pals then spent much of the rest of the movie showing monks as drunken clowns, bishops as corrupt fatties, and Muslim warriors as the only modern, sensible people around. Robin's dad may have had the right idea but he was a little dim if he actually thought that forced conversion was what the Crusades were all about – forced conversion was expressly forbidden by Christianity and there was hardly any concerted attempt to convert Muslims in the Holy Land. Christians were always in a minority, and the Crusaders assumed that this would always be the case and never tried to make it otherwise. Neither Robin nor Robin's dad, of course, has the final word on early medieval geopolitics and religious conflict but this and so many other movies, television shows, and novels stress an absurdity that has become common belief: that what is now Israel, Palestine, Syria, Lebanon, Jordan, and the surrounding area was somehow content, peaceful, and righteous before and until European knights invaded and did what, we are also told, European knights always did – raped, pillaged, destroyed, murdered, and so on.

The Crusades were never imperialism as we know it in any modern form; the region had been strongly Christian long before it was conquered by Islamic cavalry; Christendom was provoked over and over again by vehement and highly aggressive Muslim expansion; the Crusades were barely acknowledged in the Islamic world until the late nineteenth century because the Muslims thought them largely irrelevant; cruelty did occur but was nowhere near as common or extreme as is usually suggested; and Islam was rarely as tolerant and pluralistic as its apologists both within and outside its religion and culture now claim. The rest of this book will show that with abundant examples. I sincerely wish it were not the case.

It's important that we spend some time on this subject because it shapes so much of the modern conversation. First we need to establish what the Crusades were and when they happened. Let's deal with the chronology of the Crusades first. They began in 1095 when Pope Urban II made a preaching tour through France; what we know as the First Crusade took place between 1096 and 1102, with the capture of Jerusalem by the Christians from the Muslims happening in the summer of 1099. Because Jerusalem needed support from neighbouring areas, other Christian settlements were established in Antioch, Tripoli, and Edessa, and all these were aided by military intervention throughout the first half of the twelfth century, with the Second Crusade taking place between 1147 and 1149. Crusades were not, however, confined to the Holy Land in this period and also took place in Spain, Germany, the Baltic, Poland, Bohemia, and even against enemies of the papacy in Italy, but these do have the popular resonance and are not clouded in the same mythology and fallacy as the struggles in Palestine, for all sorts of modern political, emotional, and theological reasons.[7]

Jerusalem and most of the region fell to the Muslim leader Saladin in 1187. While the Third Crusade (1189–92) and the German Crusade (1197–98) recaptured much that was lost, the city of Jerusalem remained in Islamic hands. There were popular and largely non-military expeditions: in 1212, the Children's Crusade; in 1251, the Crusade of the Shepherds; and then military campaigns with the Fourth Crusade (1202–1204), which was diverted to Constantinople; and the Fifth Crusade (1217–29), which resulted in the temporary recapture of Jerusalem until it was lost again in 1244. The Fifth Crusade captured Jerusalem but the Moslems had destroyed the walls before the arrival of the Crusader army, so the Christians were unable to hold it once the Crusader army returned to Europe. Frederick II, the Holy Roman Emperor, led the Sixth Crusade. He made a treaty with the Moslems in 1229 whereby Jerusalem would be handed over to the Christians. The treaty lasted ten years, and in 1244 Jerusalem was once again conquered by the Moslems. Other Crusader campaigns were launched by the French in the 1260s and 1280s, and Crusader armies also entered Egypt and Tunisia at various times in the thirteenth century. In 1309 and 1320, there were further Crusades and numerous smaller campaigns in the eastern Mediterranean. Crusading continued in different forms and sometimes as crusading leagues right up until the sixteenth century – including the great victory at Lepanto in 1571 – and the wars in the late seventeenth century to recover large parts of the Balkans from the Turks.

These were most certainly not colonial wars, and anybody who assumes that they were some sort of early Western imperialism clearly has no idea about either the Crusades or about Western, or for that matter Eastern, imperialism. The purpose of empire is to make money and extend power by controlling the economy and resources of a foreign country and culture, by exploiting its people and increasing the influence of the imperial power. The Crusades were not profitable for the Crusaders and actually bankrupted many noble families due to the enormous cost of arming a knight and his retinue and maintaining them in a land so far away from France, England, or Germany. If money was the intention, far easier pickings could be found in Europe or even within a home country, what with profit from a ransom of an enemy or the capture of fertile land. There was hardly any attempt during the campaigns to use the local economy to enrich Europe, and the Muslim population tended to continue its financial, working, and business life as it had done before, often in fact making more money due to the need on the part of the European population for supplies. Just as there was no serious, concerted attempt to convert Muslims to Christianity, there was no serious attempt to use them as an imperial workforce. A few historians and far more uninformed commentators have claimed that Crusaders were the sons of poor aristocratic families desperately in need of cash who were sent to the Holy Land for plunder and that these men, often the clan failures, tended to be more violent and unscrupulous than even their brothers back home. There was never very much evidence to support this claim, and modern scholarship shows the contrary – the knights were often the cream of European chivalric society and their loss devastated their host nations. Unlike the Muslim war on Christians and Christianity that so dominates the Islamic world in the twenty-first century, the Crusades were not about expunging Islam from the region or destroying the followers of Muhammad.

A more difficult question than when they were is what the Crusades actually were. At heart they were wars of penitence, armed pilgrimages by Christians fighting for a specifically Christian cause – to regain Christian holy places, Christian shrines, and once Christian states and liberate and protect Christian people. It was all done with the certain knowledge that what they were doing was holy and just and was the right thing to do – the latter because the Crusades seemed to fulfil the demands of a just war, which was and is based on three fundamentals: the first being as a response to unjustified aggression, the second being a war on the orders of a legitimate government or authority, and the third being a conflict undertaken with the right intentions and with moral behaviour in the course of that war. What they were not were the caricatures of modern imagination, which have their origins as late as in the nineteenth century and two rather different works of literature – Sir Walter Scott's 1825 novel *The Talisman* and Joseph François Michaud's *History of the Crusades*, published in six volumes between 1812 and 1822.

Scott's historical novels were almost all a mingling of romance and fantasy with, at best, only one foot tenuously placed in genuine historical understanding. Sometimes the man lost his balance completely! Nothing wrong with that as long as they are read for fun as picturesque period pieces and little if anything more. The problem with *The Talisman* – the story of a Scottish knight on the Third Crusade, of his lady love, of Saladin as a noble soul who actually cures Richard the Lion Hearted, and of brave but vulgar and primitive Crusaders battling far more urban and enlightened Muslims – was not that it was horribly inaccurate but that it was devoured by one of the most credulous and unstable rulers in early twentieth-century Europe. Kaiser Wilhelm II of Germany was raised on Scott by his English mother and took historical romances far more seriously than was altogether appropriate. Then again, he was a bit of a clown, but a clown in charge of the most powerful army in the world. When he visited Damascus in 1898, the Kaiser made an absurdly grand, Wagneresque pilgrimage to Saladin's tomb, thus leading some of the most influential Muslims to wonder why they, rather a Christian monarch from Europe, had not fully realized Saladin's greatness. It's difficult to believe it after the century of revisionism and mythology around Saladin that has so lionized the man but from his death until the early 1900s he had been largely forgotten by the Islamic world.

Michaud's massive and massively flawed history took an entirely different approach from that of the novelist Scott. Michaud was a French nationalist and royalist who studied and understood the Crusades through the prism of the recent and contemporary French experience. The French, he wrote, had not only led the Crusades but had benefited from them and were duty-bound to continue the spirit of their medieval adventure throughout history. It was the nation's destiny, he said. Part of his analysis was entirely accurate but he mistakenly believed, and stressed, that the Crusades were a pursuit of empire and that France should still be an imperial power and increase the size and scope of its empire. A Gallic place in the sun. This was not only extraordinarily anachronistic but it was dreadful history and encouraged the French and a French empire in southeast Africa, North Africa, and the Middle East in a way that the Crusaders would never have understood. Encouraged by the French model, other European states looked to their Crusading past, and nationalists in Scandinavia, Germany, and England also adopted the atavistic Crusading memory, many of them assuming that every European intervention abroad was somehow in the direct tradition of medieval knights. They never were.

This twisting of history by Europeans inevitably began to bleed into the Muslim understanding of the Crusades, an understanding that, contrary to what we think today, had little or no historical significance. Since the 1980s in particular, we have heard Islamic extremists and even some relative moderates speak of "Crusaders" when they describe Western governments and their armies, and this implies a long-established Muslim perception of Christendom and its secular successors. Not so. Until the end of the nineteenth century, the Crusades had been largely forgotten, and when they were considered it was in the context of a great Islamic triumph over the forces of alien Christianity. Rather than assuming themselves to be victims and weak, Muslims viewed the Crusades through the image of victory and strength. All this changed in the 1890s as the Turkish Ottoman Empire, the sick man of Europe who refused to consult a doctor, was disintegrating under economic decline, nationalist resentment and rebellion, and an archaic rule that had not kept pace with the new idea of western Europe and North America. The Turkish leader Sultan Abdulhamid II quite cynically embraced pan-Islamicism and offered himself as the leader of a new caliphate to unite the entire Muslim world. The idea required an enemy, and what better than the notion that the Europe that was infringing on the Ottoman Empire was dedicated to some new crusade as a replica of the medieval original. The European powers that were threatening the Sultan's empire, of course, had little concern for religion and had abandoned Christians several times in the century when a Turkish alliance was in their interests – Britain and France, for example, had, as we saw earlier, joined with Turkey against Russia during the Crimean War. The new conflict between Europe and the Ottoman Empire and the Turkish decline were far more about geopolitics, power, money, and trading than they were about messiahs and prophets.

But this new language of victimhood found an eager

audience in the Islamic world, particularly after the publication in 1899 of the first history of the Crusades by a Muslim scholar, Sayyid 'Ali al-Hariri, and this false victimhood has done an enormous amount to enable contemporary Islamic persecution and to make it somehow beyond criticism by many in the non-Islamic world.

At the same time this book was published, many young Arabs were travelling to Europe for an education and learning from their liberal European colleagues, who had embraced the fashionable views of the Crusades, that the Muslims had been wronged and oppressed. Today the narrative of the Muslim world is that what the Christians failed to achieve a thousand years ago, they now try to accomplish through other and sometimes the same means.

The entire thesis is absurd on any number of levels but the Western world is too timid in its self-identity and confidence and too bathed in political correctness to aggressively contradict the argument. More than this, self-styled Western intellectuals and journalists seem to confirm Islamic fears, misusing the word *Crusades* and having even less understanding of and just as much hatred for Christianity and Christian history as the shapers of Muslim opinion. There is some excuse for the Muslim attitude, little for the Western one. The general view in the West in particular is that the Crusades were so wrong that even the Pope apologized for them. Actually, he didn't. On the first Sunday of Lent in the year 2000, Pope John Paul II led a day of pardon and repentance in which he asked "forgiveness from the Lord for the sins, past and present, of the sons and daughters of the Church." The Crusades were not mentioned but a statement was made concerning contrition for "sins committed in the service of truth."

The Crusades were a response to a plea from the terrified population of the Christian lands of the East, mostly Eastern Orthodox, whose cities and countries were being invaded by the Seljuk Turks. This Islamic expansion was nothing new and had begun almost as early as Islam itself. The Middle East, North Africa, the Levant, and the neighbouring and surrounding areas were by the fifth century heavily Christian, with many of the Church Fathers and leaders of the Church coming from and living in the region. There were Christian and pagan minorities but, obviously, no Muslims because Mohammad was not even born until around the year 570. Yet as early as 638, Islamic armies had conquered Jerusalem, and they went on to occupy most of North Africa by the end of the century. They had conquered Spain by 711, and it was only the victory of Charles Martel at Tours and Poitier in 732 that halted what was then seen as the seemingly unstoppable Muslim domination of Europe. The centre of Eastern Christianity in Constantinople retained parts of its empire but had lost Palestine, Syria, and North Africa and hundreds of thousands of Christians to war, execution, and forced conversion.

Naturally a number of Christians, Jews, and others voluntarily embraced Islam, but the image of an entire non-Muslim world suddenly pleading to become Muslim is, frankly, absurd. Conversion and cultural and theological shift were largely the results of military dominance, and a change of religion took place out of fear and a disappointing but understandable desire to become part of the clearly ascendant group within the area. Enormous numbers of Christians refused to become Muslim and experienced varying degrees of tolerance and oppression in the new Islamic empire – at best their state of dhimmitude, a protected but controlled usually Christian or Jewish minority within an Islamic state, gave them relative security but kept them in a humiliating condition where they were second-class citizens required to pay a special tax, be subservient to their Muslim compatriots, and be restricted in how they could maintain churches and conduct their religious life. There seems to be a campaign today to portray Islamic countries in the medieval age as islands of pluralism and co-existence in an otherwise cruel, intolerant, and Christian ocean. Such wrong-headed revision leads to drowning, not swimming.

By the eleventh century, the Arab Empire had divided into three separate areas of rule, based in Spain, Egypt, and Iraq and Persia. The Fatimid dynasty in Egypt had control of Jerusalem, and by 1027 Constantinople had managed to secure various rights and privileges from Egypt for the Christians of the city most sacred to Christianity – Jerusalem is only the third holiest place in Islam – and guaranteed the safety of pilgrims from Europe who made the always dangerous journey to the city. This changed with the coming of the Seljuk Turks, who first took Christian Armenia and then all of Anatolia, defeating the armies of Eastern Christianity in 1071 at the battle of Manzikert. The emperor Alexios Komnenos took over a decaying Eastern empire and managed to halt the decline, partly by coming to terms with a papacy that had previously been viewed with deep suspicion by Orthodox Christians. This new relationship led directly to an armed intervention by Catholic Europe when the persecution of Christians and attacks on Christian pilgrims became unbearable. Thus began the Crusades. They were a response to the Islamic conquest of Christian lands and Christian peoples, and in many ways it is remarkable that Christian armies did not take action sooner. Today we are incredulous that this should have happened; it says a great deal about the time and the facts that the Crusades did not come as a surprise to the Muslims, who intended to take all of Christian Europe as well as the Christian East and would try to do so for centuries to come. They had expected a Christian response for decades.

Were the Crusades brutal, were they justified by Christian thought, were they unique in the medieval world? They certainly were brutal, in that warfare and battle were brutal in the Middle Ages, but then military clashes are seldom peaceful and loving and are not supposed to be. War is bloody, nasty, and brutish, and never more so than in the great atheist twentieth century when God-hating and religion-hating military dictators such as Hitler and Stalin murdered tens of millions. The Crusades were certainly of the time. Cities that refused to surrender were usually sacked, and enemies who fought on after quarter was offered were often killed. The Crusaders treated their Muslim enemies as they treated their Christian enemies at home in Europe and exactly how they expected to be treated – and were – by their Muslim enemies in the Middle East. Remember, the Pope finally responded to pleas from the Eastern Christian empire after years of persecution and violence. Pope Innocent III wrote, "How does a man love according to divine precept his neighbour as himself when, knowing that his Christian brothers in faith and in name are held by the perfidious Muslims in strict confinement and weighed down by the yoke of heaviest servitude, he does not devote himself to the task of freeing them? . . . Is it by chance that you do not know that many thousands of Christians are bound in slavery and imprisoned by the Muslims, tortured with innumerable torments?"

The taking of Jerusalem in 1099 has also been depicted as a uniquely shocking moral and literal bloodbath – men walking knee-deep in gore and thousands of bodies torn apart in the streets in the city where Christ walked. The great success of the Crusades, the capture of Jerusalem, the story runs, also reflected the inherent violence of the Crusaders and their cause. History is not usually quite as clear and polarized between good and bad as that. The Crusaders were deeply spiritual and religious people, but today we might interpret some of that religiosity as superstition and credulity – they were convinced that when they finally reached Jerusalem having fought so many fierce and costly battles, the city and the Holy Sepulchre within it would be given to them by God without any resistance. In fact the Fatimids had won Jerusalem back from the Turks a year earlier, and these Muslims, as opposed to the Turks, would almost certainly have come to an agreement with the Crusaders to allow Christian access to holy places and sites of pilgrimage, as they had done in the past. Be that as it may, the latest rulers of the city refused to surrender when the Crusaders arrived, and adopted the standard defensive positions of a besieged force. There were days of prayer and fasting from the Christian armies and even a heavily mocked barefoot march around Jerusalem in the hope that such a gesture would please God and lead the walls of the city to collapse. Lack of shoes failed but the presence of siege towers, catapults, and a massive battering ram was far more effective. The Crusaders broke through on July 15, 1099.

What happened next does not make for comfortable reading and the same applies to any account of a taken city in the medieval period. Many defenders were killed. Muslims who took shelter in the al-Aqsa mosque were slaughtered. As repugnant as this was, they were combatants who had been trying to kill Crusaders just an hour before. The Christian soldiers were out of control, which was again a frequent occurrence in sieges in the Middle Ages: the combination of relief after constant fear of death, the desire for revenge on those who had killed friends and colleagues, the lust for food and water, the unleashing of the basest of animal instincts that exist within man. The actions were not organized, and we know from Hebrew sources found in Cairo that prisoners were taken to Ashkelon, where they were ransomed. The same sources also record the respect shown toward Muslim women by the Crusaders and note that this was not typical of other battles that had taken place in the Holy Land. We also know that wholesale massacre could not have occurred because as well as the ransoming of prisoners a number of Muslims were expelled – a source as unsympathetic as Saladin himself proves this because he discovered the descendants of the Jerusalem garrison in Damascus, where their parents had fled after being removed by the Crusaders and sent to Syria. Expulsions of people thought to be dangerous and opposed to the government was, again, typical if not desirable. Christians, for example, had been systematically purged from the city by the Fatimids before the Crusaders arrived. Prisoners, however, were certainly killed and so were some women and children, and even if this was out of fear because an Arab army was in the region and the Christians were frightened of leaving Jerusalem with a small guard and a large Muslim population, it still does not justify the killing of the defeated.

So what are we to conclude about the Crusades? They were not the proudest moment of Christian history but nor were they the childish caricature of modern Western guilt and certainly not that of contemporary Muslim paranoia. Most Christians feel shame about what happened and apologize for wrongs that occurred but it is almost unheard of for Islamic leaders offering any form of contrition for the Islamic conquest of the Christian heartlands of the Middle East. The impulse generally does not exist in a Muslim people told by their scholars that the Crusades were uniquely evil and anti-Muslim, especially when this attitude is enabled or empowered by Western anti-Christians. Indeed it is not uncommon in radical Islamic circles today to hear of calls for a re-conquest of Spain, let alone the establishment of a Muslim theocracy in the entire Middle East.

That Christians in Pakistan, Nigeria, Indonesia, and the Maldives – so far away from the Middle East – should suffer today in part due to a false history based to a degree on a misunderstanding of an early medieval conflict is horrible. That Christians in the Middle East, who are Arab and indigenous and have nothing to do with Europe or the Crusaders, should also be persecuted is similarly dreadful. The Crusades are really part of an enormous campaign of excuse and denial, an aspect of an Islamic radicalism that uses paranoia and a contrived past to try to justify modern wrongdoings and hatreds. This is all setting and context for what we are now about to describe, some of the reasons why the situation is what it is.

SYRIA AND IRAQ

IN MARCH 2014, I interviewed Sister Hatune Dogan, a Turkish-born nun who is a member of the Universal Syrian Orthodox Church under the Holy See of Antioch. She and her family were forced to leave Turkey when she was a young girl because of Islamic persecution, and they found safety and refuge in Germany. She studied theology and psychotherapy in her adopted country and is now an accomplished, multi-lingual woman who has toured the world extensively and seen humanity at its finest as well as worst. She has travelled throughout the Islamic world, partly to expose the persecution of Christians and to try to ease their plights. She has spent particular time in recent years in Iraq and, most recently, in Syria. As much as she has seen many examples of atrocity and suffering over the years and is hardened and experienced, the fate of Syrian Christians has shocked her.

"I met with a man who had gone out one morning to tend his fields. He did so in all innocence, as part of his daily routine. He suddenly looked up and saw a body, then another, then another. All of them with their heads cut off. He looked to the next field and then to the next and realized there were hundreds of murdered and decapitated people, all of them Christians. He still shakes even now when he describes the experience because of the trauma," she told me.[1]

She paused, trying to control the speed and clarity of her speech, English not being her first language. "There are slaughterhouses, many slaughterhouses, in Syria where Christians are taken to be tortured and slaughtered. People who are not political, who do not choose or take sides in the conflict, are taken from their families, kidnapped, forced to deny their faith and then – whether they have or not – are killed, often by beheading. This is not about siding with the government, not about siding with President Assad, but about sheer persecution of a peaceful but vulnerable minority. Yet the world says so little, and often nothing at all. I have been lied about because I speak out, accused of being an Assad puppet. No, no, no! I simply want to tell the world of what Christians are having to suffer at the hands of radical Islam."

What has occurred in Syria to Christians in particular in the past two years has been appalling and is all the more horrifying because Syria has been for many years one of the few places in the Arab world where Christians enjoyed something approaching equality. Ruled by an Arab nationalist rather than an Islamic ideology, and by the Ba'ath party under Hafez al-Assad and then his British-educated son Bashar Hafez al-Assad, Syria with its more than 2.5 million Christians, was a relatively modern, secular if heavily controlled and policed state. The Assads ruled despotically, were often oppressive and not at all democratic or liberal in any genuine sense, but sharia law did not dominate the body politic, and Assad, himself part of a Muslim minority sect, gave individual Christians positions of authority and responsibility, protected Christian communities, and tried to – at least within an Arab, Islamic context – achieve a relative separation of mosque and state. This is not in any way to paint Assad's Syria as some pluralistic paradise, but for Christians it was, relatively speaking, a place of freedom in which to live, to work, and to worship. The largest Christian communities are in Aleppo, Damascus, and Homs but Christians live – or lived – throughout the country. Syria claims not to have a state religion but the president has to be a Muslim and the various Christian churches – Eastern Orthodox, Eastern Rite Catholic, and various minority groups – are well aware of the limits to their rights and freedoms.

Writing in Britain's *Catholic Herald* newspaper in June 2013, Father Alexander Lucie-Smith summed up the situation rather well. "When I visited Syria, Bashar's father was still in power, and he and his two sons' portraits were everywhere. (The elder of the sons, Basil, was dead by that time.) These triple portraits were referred to as 'The Blessed Trinity' by the people I knew. They did not care for the personality cult around the Assad family, but one had the impression that this was the price they had to pay, albeit with some reluctance, if they wanted to live in a peaceful and secular Syria. A Bishop spoke to me about Bashar Al-Assad some years later. The Catholic bishops had had a meeting with the President on his accession and asked him about their pipe dream, opening a Catholic University in Damascus. Bashar was sympathetic, but said he could not allow it, on the grounds that if he were to allow a Catholic University, he would have to allow all religions to open confessional universities. Without anything being said, they all knew what that would mean: extremism and fragmentation.

"Yes, it was the stability of the graveyard; and it was an economic timewarp, full of American cars from the 1950's; but it was happy country as far as I could see, and a beautiful one, and a country at peace. My friends in Aleppo who were so good to me when I visited them, are now praying and hoping for an Assad victory. Can you blame them? The Christians of Syria have no real choice in the matter. They have been a tolerated, indeed a privileged, minority under the Ba'athist regime (as they were in Iraq); if the regime falls, their fate will be that of Iraq's Christians. They cannot understand, indeed are completely bewildered by, what I told them, namely that the British government is considering arming their enemies. They pray that this will not happen, and so do I."[2]

But now all of that has changed dramatically and disastrously. Civil unrest had begun in Syria in March 2011 and within months that unrest had become full-scale civil war. There was certainly much in the Assad regime that was deserving of opposition, and there were elements within the coalition that opposed the government that were secular, progressive, and accepting of Christianity's place in Syrian society. Sadly, there were also many Islamic fundamentalists who were the precise opposite in beliefs and in aspiration. During the Syrian conflict, around a thousand Christians have been killed and almost half a million displaced or exiled, many of them fleeing to Turkey and Lebanon, where they are not welcomed but are at least not in immediate danger of massacre. Part of the dark irony of all this is that many Iraqi Christians, whose plight is described later in this chapter, fled to Syria in the past decade to escape the Islamic persecution and violence that was rampant in their homeland. Their peripatetic existence now continues as they look to anywhere and anyone for safety. Syrian Christians have been killed, Syrian churches have been destroyed, Syrian Christian culture has been effectively ruined. Although estimates are difficult to establish, it seems that at least eighty-five churches have been burned to the ground, vandalized beyond use, or bombed into rubble by Islamic militias. Entire towns, such as the town of Ma'loula, have been raided.

It is entirely reasonable to argue that Ma'loula is historic and iconic in the Middle East and in the wider Christian world. The town has a large and ancient Christian population, one of the very few left in existence that speaks a Western Neo-Aramaic used by Jesus Christ. In other words, these people speak the language of their Messiah. By ethnicity they are Assyrian/Syriac, established in the area long before the birth of Islam and the Arab invasions, and even the Muslims whom they live alongside are pre-Arab, indigenous and local people who embraced Islam rather than immigrants or invaders who brought their Muslim faith with them. Built high and into the mountainside and a little less than sixty kilometres from Damascus, this unique town is a living memorial to the longevity and resilience of Middle Eastern Christianity and a thriving, living community in itself. For some months, Islamic terrorists connected to al-Qaeda and part of the al-Nusra Front had been entrenched close by and had attacked local Christians when they came into contact with them, or tried to prevent Christian farmers from working in nearby fields.

Then, on September 4, 2013, a concerted jihadist attack began. It started when a suicide bomber from Jordan drove his truck into a Syrian army checkpoint guarding the village. This was not merely a lone attack on government forces but the planned signal for a mass and concerted attack on the Christian town. Islamic militia quickly overran the checkpoint and killed eight soldiers, destroyed tanks, and established a military headquarters in the Safit hotel in Ma'loula. They used the hotel as a base from which to fight against Syrian forces trying to recapture Ma'loula but also poured down gunfire on the Christian community living close by. The army counterattacked but after initial successes was driven out by additional jihadist fighters.

Once in control, the Islamic groups killed many Christians, destroyed their homes, set fire to a church, and tried to and sometimes were successful in forcing local Christians to convert to Islam on fear of being beheaded if they refused. After further attacks and counterattacks, the town was restored to government control but will never be what it was and what it had been for so many centuries. Also, during the last jihadist attack, twelve nuns from the Greek Orthodox monastery of Mar Takla were kidnapped, to be exchanged two months later for what the government claims were 25, and the jihadists 150, Islamic militia prisoners. All this was a specific attack on Syrian Christianity, with no concern for the politics of the population or the wider campaign against President Assad.

An aspect of the attack that was not often reported in the media was the way the Islamist invaders tried to remove not only the Christians but the Christianity from the town, a phenomenon that is common now when Islamism expands in the Middle East and in the greater Muslim world. It is not enough that Christians should leave, convert, or die but all traces of Christianity should be removed as well. In Ma'loula there was an actual, physical attempt to change the architectural history, with churches attacked and sometimes destroyed and monuments and shrines obliterated. The statue of Christ the Saviour at the entrance of the St. Thecla Convent and the statue of the Virgin Mary close to the Safir hotel were both blown up, even when the destruction exposed the jihadists to direct fire from the Syrian army. This was a cause more important to the Muslim militia than life itself. On a more mercenary level, while numerous artifacts and relics were simply smashed, others were evidently sold abroad, because some have been directly traced to sales elsewhere in the Middle East and in Europe.

Raymond Ibrahim is the author of *Crucified Again: Exposing Islam's New War on Christians* and a regular if controversial monitor of the plight of Christians in the Islamic world. He is controversial because much of what he says and writes makes the complacent feel acutely uncomfortable. Writing in early 2014 he stated, "The worst Christian massacre – complete with mass graves, tortured-to-death women and children, and destroyed churches – recently took place in Syria, at the hands of the U.S.-supported jihadi 'rebels'; the massacre took place in Sadad, an ancient Syriac Orthodox Christian habitation, so old as to be mentioned in the Old Testament. Most of the region's inhabitants are poor, as Sadad is situated in the remote desert between Homs and Damascus (desert regions, till now, apparently the only places Syria's Christians could feel secure; 600 Christian families had earlier fled there for sanctuary from the jihad, only to be followed by it). In late October, the U.S-supported 'opposition' invaded and occupied Sadad for over a week, till ousted by the nation's military. Among other atrocities, 45 Christians – including women and children – were killed, several tortured to death; Sadat's 14 churches, some ancient, were ransacked and destroyed; the bodies of six people from one family, ranging from ages 16 to 90, were found at the bottom of a well. The jihadis even made a graphic video (with English subtitles) of those whom they massacred, while shouting Islam's victory-cry, 'Allahu Akbar.' What happened in Sadad is the most serious and biggest massacre of Christians in Syria in the past two and a half years."[3]

There are critics who argue that while conditions are certainly severe for Syrian Christians, tales of forced conversions and slaughterhouses are apocryphal or at least exaggerated. The weight of opinion, however, seems to be on the side of those who claim that conditions are quite as bad as is claimed, and some of the confusion is a result of the understandable desire for some Christians – both in Syria and elsewhere – to play down the atrocities and persecution in an attempt to build ecumenical bridges or merely prevent angry reactions from jihadists and thus further violence. If so, it doesn't seem to be having the desired effect. The so-called slaughterhouses have been described numerous times by reliable witnesses and the violence continues.

Walid Shoebat and his son Theodore Shoebat have been criticized by some for being overly condemning of Islam and the Muslim treatment of Christians, but their research is thorough and even the critical have not come forward to reasonably and reliably critique what they wrote about an almost unimaginable level of horror in Syria in March 2014:

"Saif Al-Adlubi told the story when the Egyptian butcher would examine the row of people who were waiting their execution. Al-Adlubi witnessed at least two Armenians who were waiting their turn to be slaughtered since no one paid their ransom, the sum of $100,000 each. 'He grabbed the neck of one elderly Armenian Christian,' says Al-Adlubi, which the Egyptian butcher was about to slaughter. The Egyptian butcher felt the neck of the Christian Armenian saying 'you're an aged man and your neck is soft and I don't have to sharpen my knife for you.' Others might be more difficult depending on their physique. Saif Al-Adlubi tells of his miraculous escape to the Turkish village of Rehaniyeh from Syria. He was probably one of the few survivors who sounded the alarm on one of the gruesome systematic human extermination centers carried out by the Takfiri Jihadist group ISIS. The prison centers where the ISIS (Da'ish) controls have become miniatures of what was during the Nazi SS extermination camps, except the ISIS carries out the extermination in a much more horrific way. Da'ish transforms the prisons into kangaroo courts with systematic slaughterhouses and killing centers to exterminate Christians and Muslims who disagree with the Takfiri ideology. Once they are found guilty, the way they deal with the victims was as if they were cattle. The ISIS stands for The Islamic group of Iraq and Syria. ISIS is also known in Middle East circles as Da'ish. Rescue Christians obtained footage of another slaughterhouse from one Syrian Christian named Kamil Toume to confirm the claims."[4]

Dali is a young woman who fled with her family from Syria to Jordan and then to Britain, where she agreed to be interviewed on condition of anonymity because, as she explained, her grandparents still lived in Syria. "The old feel more of an attachment to the land and the soil," she explained, looking and sounding as modern and Western as any of the students in the university common room where we met. "They believe that leaving Syria would be a betrayal of their history, their clan, and also of their religion. It's as though they think of exile as a form of betrayal of Christ, which is something we young people don't quite understand. I pleaded with them, told them their deaths would achieve nothing, but there's a sense of acceptance, almost calmness or even complacency I suppose, about that generation. It's also so hard, so challenging, so dramatic for them to leave and start again. A lot of us could already speak English but not the older people. What hurts me so much is the unfairness of it all, and that it's very likely I will never see them again." She turned her head to hide her tears.

"People in the West imagine we lived in some sort of biblical scene, like a silly movie about the desert and Arabs and camels. I grew up in a wealthy town on the edge of a big city, with a large television, surround sound, a new laptop, modern clothes, freedom. Honestly, I never felt as a Christian or a woman that I was threatened. I do remember as a child when we went to Christmas mass there would be soldiers outside, before and during and after, but they were there to make sure we were safe and it made us feel good and secure. I know Assad did terrible things, I'm not an idiot, but as soon as the war started, the life that I had, that we had, disappeared in what seemed like just a few weeks. When a friend of my father was shot dead by terrorists, we decided to leave and thank God we had enough money and connections to get out. Not everybody could."[5]

She paused, collected herself, and then looked more determined, even angry, than at any other time in the interview. "For me the turning point was a girl who I had known since we were tiny. We'd played together, I knew her mum and dad. Sure I knew she was Sunni Muslim but we didn't care and I didn't think she cared about me being a Christian. I'd never seen her wearing covering before but there she was with her head and most of her body covered and she came to find me. 'I've always hated you and now I can tell you so,' she said. 'You don't belong here. The Jews, the Crusaders, the Americans, the British, the Christians, you don't belong here. Go, go!' Sometimes I think she was right."

The litany of violence and pain is indeed breathtaking, even if we look at a mere two-year period. I will not elaborate but merely recount the attacks. The list is not extensive and could be far longer. In January 2012, three Christians were killed in Damascus in planned attacks, two of them while waiting to buy bread for their family. The following month in

Qusayr, Sunni terrorists stopped a family car at gunpoint, forced the father of the family out of the vehicle, murdered him in front of his wife and children, and then executed the children. In July in Jaramana, a car bomb killed and injured dozens of Christians in a heavily Christian neighbourhood of the town. In August in Zamalka, seven Christians, all members of the same family, were killed by Liua Islam. Three of the victims were children. In the same month in Jaramana, a Christian funeral was attacked by a car bomb planted by a Sunni group, killing twenty-seven people.[6]

In October 2012, three Christians were murdered by Muslims in Said Naya, and later in the month in Qatana an orthodox priest was tortured and murdered. When his body was found, it was discovered that his eyes had been gouged out. He had been trying to negotiate the release of Christian prisoners at the time of his murder. A few days later in Damascus, thirteen Christians were killed on their way to church in Damascus; then a car bomb in Deir ez-Zor killed five Christians outside of their church. Also in October 2012 in Jaramana, twelve Christians were killed in a bomb attack. Similar attacks had occurred in Aleppo and Ras al-Ayn – in the latter in December 2012, a heavily pregnant woman was widowed when her husband, a thirty-eight-year-old taxi driver named Andrei Arbashe, was beheaded and his body left to be eaten by wild dogs. Sister Agnes-Mariam de la Croix knew Arbashe: "His only crime was his brother criticized the rebels, accused them of acting like bandits, which is what they are. . . . The uprising has been hijacked by Islamist mercenaries who are more interested in fighting a holy war than in changing the government. It has turned into a sectarian conflict. One in which Christians are paying a high price . . . More than 200 families were driven out in the night,' Sister Agnes-Mariam says. 'People are afraid. Everywhere the deaths squads stop civilians, abduct them and ask for ransom, sometimes they kill them."

In July 2013, the bodies of seven beheaded Christians were found in Homs. In November, a Christian section of Damascus was shelled and two people were killed. Also in November, nine Christian children were killed by debris when Islamists targeted a Christian school for mortar attack. In Sadad, six Christians, all members of a single family, were killed by Islamists. In December 2013, twelve people were killed in a church when Islamist militia attacked it because it was being used as a food distribution centre. In August 2014, in Marmarita a Christian was beheaded when he was discovered wearing a crucifix around his neck; in September 2014, a Christian was executed for refusing to convert to Islam, and the following month two Christians were kidnapped and beheaded in Deir Hassan.[7]

The terror is working. Christians have left and are leaving. The situation may improve for them but will never be the same for those whom they have left behind. The road to Damascus is now stained and soaked in blood and pain, and some of the oldest churches in the world have been destroyed or left as relics and lifeless museums of historical interest. Diasporas of Syrian Christians have now been created in North America and Europe but their homeland increasingly becomes Christian-free. It is precisely what many in the Muslim world have wanted for some time.

While in Iraq there are numerous differences compared to the Syrian situation, some of the history is eerily similar. Christians had lived in Iraq since the earliest period of the Christian story, and the community in that country is one of the oldest and most established Christian cultures and societies in history. The Chaldeans became Christian in the first century, and Iraqi Christians are still mainly ethnic Chaldeans who speak a form of Eastern Aramaic, but there are also many Assyrians, Armenians, and Kurds. Denominations are numerous, some of them ancient and some modern; they include Chaldean Catholic, Assyrian Church of the East, Syrian Orthodox, Syriac Catholic, Armenian Apostolic, Armenian Catholic, Roman Catholic, and various Protestant churches – so, an established, integral, and respected part of Iraq and the Middle East. Numbers can be difficult to establish because of fear on the part of Christians to self-identify and also due to state reluctance to give detailed information, or because some in authority want to deny the genuine size and significance of minorities. It seems, though, that by the early 1980s there were almost 1.5 million Christians in Iraq, perhaps 9 per cent of the population. Recent figures speak of less than half a million, living mainly in Baghdad, Basra, Mosul, and Arbil, and some believe that the figure is closer to a mere two hundred thousand.

Like Syria, Iraq had long been ruled by a secular form of Arab nationalism and a local version of Ba'athism. Saddam Hussein was also a despot but an even more controlling and sadistic leader than President Assad or his father. Partly as a policy of divide and conquer but also out of a genuine commitment to an Arab state that rejected Islamic fundamentalism and oppression of Arab Christians, Saddam tolerated and even protected his Christian minority when it was advantageous to him and his regime. But Iraqi Christians always lived a tenuous existence and knew they had to be watchful. Yet Saddam's deputy and effectively foreign minister for some time was Tariq Aziz, a Christian at least in name, tribe, and tradition.

With the wars in Iraq, however, and the eventual fall of the brutal dictatorship of Saddam Hussein, the various Islamic sects in the country and their foreign Islamic allies began a virtual civil war, and Christians, refusing to participate in the sectarianism and often falsely perceived as being pro-Western or even pro-Saddam, were specifically targeted by Islamic militias. It is tragic and perhaps indicative that a United States led by an evangelical Christian should lead a war in Iraq that led to the persecution and slaughter of Christians and the hemorrhage of these ancient communities of followers of Jesus Christ from the heartland and homeland of Christianity. A war fought ostensibly to keep Christians safe in Ohio and Alabama has made the lives of Christians living in Baghdad and Mosul completely unbearable.

Archdeacon Temathius Esha, a priest in Doura, a suburb of Baghdad, was quoted shortly before Christmas 2013 as saying that his town "was once one of the biggest Christian communities in Iraq, with 30,000 families. Now there are only 2,000 left. They feel they are strangers in their own land, and that makes them want to leave. The bleeding from migration is continuous. . . . [Under Saddam if] you avoided politics you could survive, but since the war we have been attacked, robbed, raped and forced out of both Doura and the country. Often just psychological pressure has been enough; people will drive past here and fire guns in the air, or leave bullets and threatening messages outside Christian homes. Sometimes Islamic extremism is used as an excuse, sometimes it's just blackmail for criminal purposes."[8]

It's a familiar scene and sight and there are few indications that any of this will this change. Writing in Britain's *Daily Telegraph*, Colin Freeman stated, "Those unable to join Iraqi diasporas in Europe and America often fled to sister communities in neighbouring Syria, only to find themselves in similar peril thanks to al-Qaeda's presence in the war against President Bashar al-Assad. In post-Mubarak Egypt, the Christians fear a similar reckoning, and only last month Pope Francis warned that the entire Church was in peril across the region, adding: 'We will not resign ourselves to imagining a Middle East without Christians.' Yet with al-Qaeda once again on the rise in Iraq – more than 6,000 people have been killed in 2013, the most in five years. . . .

"The invasion of 2003 – portrayed by some as a 'Crusade' by fellow Christians – led to little in the way of direct reprisals. However, in the lawless years that followed, their prosperity made them targets for kidnappers and criminals, who sometimes felt less guilty preying on non-Muslims. Almost uniquely in Iraq, Christians have no tribal structure, depriving them of the blood ties under which other Iraqis bind together in times of trouble. As such, they have never formed self-defence militias, despite the fact that post-war Iraq offers little reward to those who turn the other cheek. . . . As al-Qaeda's presence in Iraq has grown, Christians have been targeted deliberately, with sporadic bombings of churches and killings of priests."[9]

Once again, the list of attacks makes for terrible and depressing reading, and this is merely a partial chronicle and covers only a short period. Please read it while remembering that each one speaks of a person, a family, a community, and a country. The pain and anguish is almost beyond comprehension and their blood cries out. The year 2010 saw attacks throughout Iraq. In November and December in Baghdad, Mosul, and Dujail, there were repeated killings, one of the most shocking being when an elderly Christian woman was strangled in her own home. In November in Mosul, two Christian brothers were shot dead in their shop; in the same city a man and his six-year-old daughter were murdered. Mosul was also the scene of the murder of three Christian brothers. Also in November, a series of attacks in Baghdad and Mosul by bomb, gun, and mortar killed eight Christians, and in October in Baghdad forty-four Christian worshippers and seven police officers were killed when Islamic State of Iraq Fedayeen militia attacked a church service. Earlier in October in Samarra, where there had been relatively little anti-Christian violence, a convert to Christianity was killed by his son and nephew. Converts to Christianity living in heavily Muslim areas are particularly vulnerable to attacks and especially hated by Islamists. Some radical Muslims do see a place for ancient Christian communities but few if any will allow and tolerate Muslims leaving their faith for another.

Mosul was under severe attack in the early months of 2010. This beautiful city is Iraq's third largest, the centre of the Nestorian Christianity of the Assyrians and close to the ancient and biblical city of Nineveh. It also contains Old Testament tombs, including that of Jonah, and is soaked in Christian history and culture. According to local Christian leaders, that is precisely why it is so targeted by jihadists. In February a father and his two sons were murdered, a 57-year-old shopkeeper was kidnapped and then shot dead, a young Christian was shot, then a 42-year-old – another shopkeeper – shot dead and his body left in front of his business, then a 20-year-old Christian was shot while working in a store, and another business owner was killed.[10]

At the end of 2009 in Mosul, a bomb left close to an ancient church killed two people, and a thirty-year-old Christian man was shot dead on the street. The rest of the year had been just as bad. In December, four Christians were murdered when a church and Christian school were attacked in Mosul, and in the same month in Kirkuk a Christian man was carjacked, dragged from his vehicle, and killed in front of his young daughter. Earlier in the year in Baghdad, four churches were attacked simultaneously, killing four people and wounding numerous others. In Mosul, a Christian man was beheaded and a five-year-old boy murdered. In April, two elderly Christian sisters were murdered, and in March a seventy-one-year-old Christian man was killed in his own home in Kirkuk. Another man was shot dead in a restaurant in Mashtal.

In 2008, Mosul was once again the concerted target for a dozen deadly attacks. Christians were kidnapped and shot by Islamists, a leading Christian poet was murdered, a father and son were shot dead at their workplace, a Christian-owned pharmacy was raided and the owner killed, a disabled Christian man was taken from his business and murdered, a sixty-five-year-old Christian doctor and a priest were killed, and in a particularly chilling attack a group of Islamists set up a roadblock, stopped cars, and forced the occupants to identify and prove their faith. When they came across a group of Christians, they murdered them. Also in 2008, an event shook not only the Iraqi Christian community but all of Middle Eastern Christendom. Chaldean Catholic archbishop Paulos Faraj Rahho, the archbishop of Mosul, was found in a shallow grave close to the city. He had been kidnapped after leading a prayer service at the Church of the Holy Spirit in Mosul on February 29. The driver and two guards who had been with him when he was taken were certainly killed during the kidnapping and he died either then or later. The Vatican media spokesman, Father Federico

Lombardi, said: "The most absurd and unjustified violence continues to afflict the Iraqi people and in particular the small Christian community, whom the Pope holds in his prayers in this time of deep sadness. This tragic event underscored once more and with more urgency the duty of all, and in particular of the international community, to bring peace to a country that has been so tormented." Rome's reaction was, however, far too weak for an Iraqi Christian community that was crying out for strong and determined international help but invariably received token regrets and responses from foreign Christian churches that – according to many – seemed more concerned with ecumenism and not naming and offending Islam and Muslims than with protecting besieged Christians.

In December 2007 in Basra, a Christian brother and sister were killed and their bodies dumped in a garbage site, and in the same month in Mosul a young Christian girl was shot dead at the market. The entire year had seen attack after attack, with age, sex, or disability being irrelevant. In Kirkuk, two nuns, aged seventy-nine and eighty-five, were stabbed to death in their home, and a priest was kidnapped in Baghdad and was beheaded. Also in Baghdad, a bomb was placed in a heavily Christian area and sixteen people were killed. In September, there was what had become a now common occurrence when a twenty-one-year-old woman was first harassed by Muslims because she was wearing jeans and dressed in a fashion that was entirely normal in Iraq before the war. She was mobbed, beaten, and stabbed to death. A month earlier in Dura, a Christian woman was kidnapped, tortured, and beheaded.[11]

In February 2005, a suicide bomb car attack took place in Hilla, aimed not specifically at Christians but taking place after the government had specifically spoken out at anti-Christian violence and had appealed for Iraqi Christians to come forward and volunteer to serve in the Iraqi security forces. The *Guardian*, the British liberal newspaper, reported the situation as follows:

"A suicide car bomber killed more than 100 people and wounded dozens more today in an attack on a crowd in Iraq. In the deadliest incident since the end of the war, the bomber drove into people queuing outside a medical clinic in Hilla, about 60 miles south of Baghdad, police said. Major-General Osman Ali, an Iraqi National Guard commander in Hilla, put the toll at 115 dead and 132 wounded. A health official in Babil province said the death toll could rise. Dia Mohammed, the director of Hilla General hospital, said most of the victims were recruits waiting to take medicals as part of the application process to join the Iraqi police and national guard. A statement distributed to reporters by the Babil province police headquarters said: 'A suicide car bomb hit a gathering of people who were applying for work in the security services.' Several people had been arrested, the statement added. Dozens of bodies lay on the ground after the blast and passers-by helped pile body parts into blankets. Piles of shoes and tattered clothes were thrown into a corner. Many of those killed had been shopping at stalls across the road from the clinic. Pools of blood could be seen on the street, and scorch marks infused with blood covered the walls of a nearby building. The blast, at 9.30am (6.30am GMT), was so powerful it nearly destroyed the suicide bomber's car, leaving only its engine partially intact."[12]

The year before, in 2004, the beheaded bodies of three people, two of them Assyrian Christians, were found dumped in a field with inscriptions from the Koran carved into their flesh. In the same year, two Arab Christians from Canada were chased by a gang of Muslims in Baghdad and beaten to death, and in the same city a forty-three-year-old Christian was killed as he left a hospital where he had been treated for injuries received during another attack by Islamists. In Bartella, a town of thirty thousand people with several historic churches and monasteries, three young Christian girls were murdered by Islamists, and several bomb attacks had earlier taken place during Christian festivals and holy days. A month earlier in Baghdad, a gang of jihadists broke into a family home and stabbed two girls, aged sixteen and six years old, to death. Also in Baghdad, four Christian workmen were killed and another injured in a morning shooting attack, and in the same Christian district another drive-by shooting, likely committed by the same group, killed another four Christians, including three women. In Basra, two Christian sisters were shot dead on their way home from a night out; their father was waiting up for their return, as he always did in case they got into trouble – the trouble he envisaged was being teased by boys or having had too much to drink.

The year 2004 was horrific but not unique. In Mosul, Sunni militia murdered an Assyrian Christian police officer, in Baghdad an Assyrian Christian married couple had their throats cut, and nearby a Muslim gang smashed their way into a home in a Christian neighbourhood and killed two children, their mother, and their grandmother. A Christian minister was also killed and four other people badly wounded when a Muslim fanatic drove his car next to the pastor and began shooting, and four women who were working in a laundry were shot dead by jihadists. The attacks were not confined to Iraqi Christians but to any Christian living or working in the country. In March, five Baptist aid workers from North Carolina, California, and Texas were in Mosul, helping to provide clean water and generally improve the lives of local people, whatever their religion. One of the team, Larry Elliott, had designed a water purification system that was so successful it was going to be used throughout Iraq. Christianity Today reported: "While driving on the east side of the city yesterday afternoon, the Baptists' car came under attack by automatic weapons fire and rocket-propelled grenades. When an off-duty Iraqi police-man found the car moments later, three of the missionaries, including Elliott and his wife, Jean, were already dead. The two wounded – another husband-and-wife team, David and Carrie McDonnall of the Dallas suburb of Rowlett – were taken to a nearby hospital. There, David McDonnall died of his wounds. His wife remains in critical condition with four gunshot wounds.

"The Elliotts were new to the mission field. David had just graduated from Southwestern Baptist Theological Seminary in 2002, Carrie was still officially a student there. In contrast, the Elliotts were longtime missionary veterans, having worked most of the last 25 years in Honduras. They were scheduled to leave Iraq later this month to close their Honduran headquar-ters and permanently relocate to Iraq. Larry Kingsley, a church deacon at the Elliotts' stateside church, told the Associated Press that the Iraq mission was more about ministering to physical needs than proclamation evangelism. 'They knew going into Iraq, they couldn't really share their Christian faith unless somebody asked them,' he said. 'They were there in a humanitarian situation. They were people who just had a great heart for helping people out.' Also killed in the attack was Karen Watson of Bakersfield, California, a single woman who con-verted to Christianity in 1997 and had recently quit her job as a detention officer to work full-time in missions."[13]

By the end of 2010 so many Christians had left Iraq that it was more difficult for Islamists to find targets and victims. Even so, the slaughter continued. In December 2011, a Christian man in Mosul was shot dead outside his home by Islamist snipers, and in the same month and the same town a Christian couple was shot dead in their car, their children surviving but suffering extensive injuries. Also in December 2011, in Zakho, thirty-two Christians were injured when Muslim mobs rioted against Christian-owned businesses. In August and September 2011, there were numerous attacks. In Kirkuk, an elderly Christian couple was gunned down; in Mosul a thirty-year-old who worked in a restaurant was killed. Shortly before this in Kirkuk, a sixty-year-old Christian man was shot dead, fourteen people were injured when a church was bombed, and another twenty-four when a Catholic church was attacked. In the early summer, a Christian man with four children was murdered by Islamists, and in Kirkuk a Christian was kidnapped, tortured, had his eyes gouged out, and was then decapitated. Mosul was hit very hard between June and August. A car bomb in a supermarket in a Christian area killed a young medical student, a woman teacher was kidnapped and her throat was cut, and a Muslim gang broke into the home of a Catholic priest, killed his father and his two brothers, and raped his mother and sister. In Baghdad in April, seven people were badly wounded when a bomb was detonated outside a church, and in the same city a seventy-year-old Christian man was stabbed to death inside his home. In January in Mosul, a Christian doctor working in a city hospital was targeted by an Islamic gang, shot, and badly wounded.

In Baghdad in March 2012, two people were killed in a bomb attack in an Orthodox church, and in the same week a group of al-Qaeda terrorists broke into another church and killed three guards. In December 2013 in Baghdad, a Christian area of a major market was attacked and eleven people were killed, and a month earlier a Christian journalist was shot dead in Mosul. A few weeks before in Mosul, a Christian woman was murdered in her own home by a Muslim gang. In the later summer in al-Tarmiyah, a Christian was kidnapped and executed, and shortly before that in Baghdad a bomb was placed outside a church, killing two people. Earlier in the summer in Baghdad, there were several attacks: two people were killed near their church, two guards were wounded when they were shot by Islamist gunmen outside a church, and a Christian-owned store was bombed, killing a father of three young children. Those Christians who are left and have courageously decided to maintain Iraqi Christianity live an extremely careful and intensely controlled existence.

In April 2014, the Chaldean patriarch of Babylon, Mar Louis Raphael I Sako, head of the Assyrian Chaldean Catholic Church, delivered a long address concerning the history of Christians and Christianity in the Middle East and in particular in Iraq. While he criticized Western intervention and imperialism and called for a just peace in Israel and Palestine, he also spoke of the reality of Christian life in modern Iraq:

"At present, there is increasingly talk of a plan to create a new Middle East. For us, it is a source of concern and fear. [Fourteen hundred] years of Islam have not been able to take us away from our lands and our churches; now Western policy has dispersed us to the four corners of the earth. More and more Christians are being victimized, and their exodus from the Middle East appears unstoppable. At present, they are estimated to be between 10 and 12 million out of a total population of 550 million, or around 3 per cent. And the pressures exerted on Christians and other religious minorities in the Middle East have increased over the past few decades, sometimes in a subtle way, in other times, openly. Discrimination, injustice, kidnapping, isolation, and intimidation have given them the impression that in many parts of the Arab-Islamic world they are doomed to extinction. All this stems from the instability of most of these countries and the growth of radical Islam, under the guise of 'political Islam.' As for the 'Arab Spring,' it lost out to extremism. 'Political' Islam wants to revive the Caliphate as much in Damascus as in Iraq! Their way of thinking and doing war is a return to the Middle Ages with Christians allowed to stay as second-class citizens!

"About half of all Iraqi Christians, once numbering a million and a half, have left the country for fear of violence and religious persecution, especially after the massacre that took place in Baghdad in 2010, in the Church of Our Lady of Salvation, and the attack in Qaraqosh against Christian students on their way to the university. Taking property away from Christians, who are deemed without rights because they are not Muslim, threatening letters sent to Christians, as well as members of other non-Muslim minorities, are making Christians feel like second-class citizens. Therefore, the question is, are the men and women who have a great and illustrious past behind them destined to disappear from Mesopotamia and the land of their ancestors?"[14]

The answer is that unless and until something changes at the most fundamental level of Islam and in the Muslim approach to religious minorities in general and Christians in particular, yes, they will disappear. Not only in Mesopotamia, but throughout the Middle East. The battle for Christian continuity in Iraq is, if we are honest, largely lost, and in Syria matters look bleak indeed. Even at its best, Christian life in Syria is now dependent on the triumph and survival of a dictator who is no genuine friend of Christianity and who has always been regarded by local Christians as a leader to be tolerated rather than embraced. Christians from both countries have fled to various countries, often to Jordan, but there is no guarantee that the Jordanian royal family with its relatively liberal religious policies will remain in power. There is, simply, nowhere else left to go in the Middle East. This is a struggle for survival and it is being lost.

EGYPT

COPTIC CHRISTIAN WEDDINGS in Egypt tend to be glorious, loud, beautiful, and grand affairs. I have attended more than one, and the sheer largesse of emotion and unbridled hospitality and sense of communal grace, lightness, and joy is irresistible. Rich or poor, the Christians of Egypt are always determined to make their weddings events to remember. As a Coptic friend once said to me after more than a few drinks, "It might be an awful marriage, but the wedding is something to remember!" It was supposed to be such an event in October 2013 on the edge of Cairo but, tragically, it was not to be. The gunmen were not heard or even noticed because of the celebrations, but as people spilled outside to celebrate, the Islamists opened fire and four people were immediately killed. Two of them were adults and two others little girls in dresses their mothers had made especially for the occasion. They were aged eight and twelve, and the large bullets ripped their small bodies apart. They died where they stood, but the two adults held on to their lives for a little longer. Many others were wounded, and the wounds were not scratches but deep stomach wounds leading to lifelong disability and limbs so shattered they necessitated amputation. Others lost eyes or suffered brain damage from head wounds. In a way, the attack was not surprising. More than forty churches had been raided by Muslim radicals since August when protest camps set up to support Muslim Brotherhood leader and former president Mohamed Morsi had been cleared by the army. Islamists blamed Christians for this and for the demise of their regime and leader, even though those Christians they scapegoated had been persecuted for generations and had no particular loyalty to either side in the divisions that so hurt modern Egypt. Their struggle was not for power but for mere existence.[1]

The reality is that to be a Christian in contemporary Egypt is to live under daily threat and constant danger; the diaspora of Egypt's Christians is a growing international phenomenon because the persecution has become even worse in recent years. This situation is profoundly worrying because there are more Christians in Egypt than in any other country in the Arab world, and although it is impossible to accurately measure the numbers, the Christian population in Egypt could be as high as 20 per cent of the total and is certainly greater than 10 per cent. Many Christians in Egypt refuse to identify themselves in surveys and questionnaires, such is their anxiety and fear. They prefer to live quietly rather than be persecuted or die loudly.

The Christian community can be traced back to the Roman era – Alexandria was one of the centres of the ancient Church – with early Christianity owing much of its life and energy to followers of Christ who lived in Egypt. The Christians of Egypt are to a large extent the closest we can get to the indigenous people of the country, but they are treated as invaders and unwanted aliens. As in so many Muslim countries, belonging and deserving depend on religion rather than citizenship, history, or identity.

Over 95 per cent of Christians in the country are members of the Coptic Church of Alexandria, an ancient and oriental church that is part of the greater international Eastern Orthodox community. Egyptian Christians also belong to the

Coptic Catholic Church and numerous evangelical and other Protestant denominations. There is also a thriving Greek Orthodox Church, the Melkite Greek Catholic Church, the Armenian Apostolic Church, the Latin Catholic or Roman Catholic Church, Armenian Catholics, Syriac Catholics, and various others. Egyptian Christians like to claim that the apostle Mark brought the faith to their country just a few years after the crucifixion and resurrection of Jesus; we have no idea if this is true but it's not beyond the realm of possibility. If it wasn't Mark who brought the Gospel to Egypt, it was very early followers of Christ, and we know for certain that Clement and Origen – both central and vital figures in the early Church and the formation of Christian theology and culture – lived in Alexandria. Egyptians converted to Christianity in large numbers and Egypt became what was effectively a Christian country with a pagan and Jewish minority.

Islam developed, as we have seen, at a much later date but did manage to transform Egypt into a Muslim nation with extraordinary speed and success, albeit always with a large and vital Christian Church existing within the Muslim majority state. There were times of relative peace and times of persecution, but the latter was never as consistent and severe as it has been for the past forty years. It's worth remembering that Jews had lived in Egypt since long before the life of Mohammad, had played a central role in Egyptian society, and were considered integral to the country's way of life. After the establishment of the state of Israel in 1948, however, they were gradually marginalized, then persecuted, and then expelled. The Jews no longer live in Egypt and their existence is generally forgotten. It will be much more difficult to expunge the Christians but the campaign is well under way.[2]

The list of attacks could fill an entire book, and while this is not the place for such an analysis, we have to consider the number of incidents and the violence of what has occurred in the past few years alone. The nature and style of government is usually irrelevant to these occurrences, and fundamentalist and alleged Muslim moderates alike have encouraged or allowed a persecution of millions of people that surely one day will be looked back upon with international shame. The last decade is the worst in recent memory. In 2004, the church at the Patmos Centre was burned down by Islamist groups within the army, killing one worshipper and injuring two others. Shortly afterwards in Taha al-Aamida, Islamists who served in the police force kidnapped three Christians working to repair a church – repairing a church is forbidden under sharia law unless specific permission has been given by the Islamic authorities. All three of the men, one of them a priest, were killed. At the beginning of 2005, a nun and her friend were stabbed outside their church in Alexandria, and a Christian minister in Cairo was killed after a prolonged campaign of threats against him and demands that he stop preaching the Gospel. At the beginning of 2006 in al-'Udaysāt, a Muslim mob attacked Christians and Christian property in a mass attack, resulting in numerous injuries and the deaths of a forty-five-year-old man and a ten-year-old child.

As was and is so often the case, these incidents are investigated in a perfunctory manner and the culprits are seldom if ever brought to justice. If, however, Christians defend themselves or retaliate, arrests, charges, trials, and imprisonment are routine. There is, in effect, a two-tier justice system in much of Egypt.

In 2006 in Alexandria, a seventy-eight-year-old man was killed and three other Christians wounded when they were attacked and stabbed by an Islamist gang outside their church. Two months later, a Christian shoemaker was knifed to death in Cairo by Islamists, and in Behma in May 2007, ten Christians were injured and forty-eight homes and seven stores were burned after the local Christian community began to turn one of their own houses into a church. In this case, the community had gone through the long and arduous process of requesting and actually being granted full authority by then president Mubarak and the state security police to perform the construction work, but the local imam, himself a state employee, refused to comply with Cairo's decision and instigated local Muslims to attack and destroy. Once again, the police intervened far too late and did little to stop the violence and arson.[3]

In 2008 in Cairo, a woman who converted to Christianity, considered especially heinous within Islam, was arrested by the police and then raped and tortured. She was released only when she agreed to return to the Islamic religion. In March 2009 in Qalubiya, a young Christian was set on fire by a Muslim mob, and his father, in his sixties, was stabbed to death. Three months later in El-Fashn, a church was invaded by a large number of Muslims, who destroyed property, pictures, and statues and assaulted twenty-two Christians who were at prayer. The year ended with the shooting death of a sixty-one-year-old man whose crime was that his son was romantically attached to a Muslim girl.

Matters did not improve in 2010. In Nag Hamadi, a fourteen-year-old and six others were murdered as they left mass; in Menoufia, a young Christian man was shot dead by a Muslim police officer – just one of many incidents in which policemen and soldiers have committed Islamist crimes and attacks. In Teleda, a minister and his wife were murdered by Islamists, enraged because a Christian had applied for permission to build a church. The pastor was not trying to convert Muslims, only trying to build a church so that his congregation would have a building in which to gather and worship. In Marsa Matruh, more than twenty Christians were badly hurt in a day of organized Islamist attacks in the town; in Cairo, a Muslim convert to Christianity was kidnapped, beaten, and managed to escape only moments before his captors were to behead him. The year ended with eleven Christians being assaulted by a Muslim group leaving their mosque after an especially vehement anti-Christian sermon.[4]

In January 2011 in Alexandria, a suicide bomb attack in a Coptic church was detonated shortly after midnight when the New Year's mass was concluding; twenty-one people were killed and more than a hundred were badly wounded. The attack was planned to cause as much damage and kill as many people as possible. The *New York Times* reported:

> By Saturday evening, patches of blood were visible high on the front walls of the church, which was pockmarked with holes. Across the street, a mosque was also stained with blood.
>
> "There were bodies on the streets," said Sherif Ibrahim, who saw the blast's aftermath. "Hands, legs, stomachs. Girls, women and men."
>
> "We're going to die here," said Mr. Ibrahim, who saw the bombing's aftermath. "But our churches are here. Our lives are here. What will we do?"[5]

What they did was leave, because the 2010 attack had the desired effect and saw the departure of a vast wave of Egyptian

Christians. This was a turning point, but still the attacks continued. In 2011 in Samalout, a Muslim policeman discharged his service revolver on a train after identifying a group of elderly Christians. A seventy-one-year-old was killed. As the police officer fired, he repeatedly cried, "Allahu Akbar" or "God is great." In Wadi el-Natroun, nineteen Christians were hurt, including two monks, when soldiers charged into a monastery, and the father of a young Christian and the father of a young Muslim were murdered because their children were dating. The local church was also burned to the ground. In April in Minya, a Christian grandmother was thrown out of her second-floor window by a Muslim gang; in the next few months in Cairo, two Christians were shot dead in a drive-by shooting, fifty Christians were injured when local Muslims threw rocks and petrol bombs at a Christian gathering, a sixty-year-old Christian was beaten to death, and two churches were firebombed and attacked by Islamists with submachine guns, killing twelve Christians. In Imbaba, a Catholic had his throat slit in church, and the sixteen-year-old nephew of the town's Catholic bishop was shot dead. In Awlad Khalaf in June, three Christians were severely injured when it was thought, wrongly, that they were trying to turn their home into a church, and the following month in Minya two Christians were killed by snipers while driving home from work. In June, six Christians, one a heavily pregnant woman, were attacked with iron rods and clubs by Muslims after a church bell was rung; in August in Minya, a Christian farmer had his throat cut by Muslims while his young son was forced to watch the slaughter. Then in Tamia a guard at a church was murdered by Muslim gunmen.

In October 2011, during the so-called revolution in Egypt, an event took place that epitomized the nuances and instability of Christian life. There were undoubtedly attempts by progressives and more secular elements in Egyptian society to develop a non-sectarian society and join Muslim and Christian young people together in opposing violence and oppression. Cairo-based journalist Yasmine El Rashidi, author of *The Battle for Egypt: Dispatches from the Revolution*, wrote in the *New York Review of Books* of the events on October 9 when members of Cairo's Coptic community marched to the Abbasiya Cathedral, headquarters of the Coptic Church.

> They prayed, as a Coptic youth leader told me, "for the day to begin and end peacefully, and for a million people to turn up" at the protest march to the State TV Building planned for that afternoon. . . .
>
> The march had been organized to protest growing attacks on churches and the lack of protection for the country's large Coptic minority under Egypt's military-backed interim government: most recently, on September 30, Muslim fanatics burned down a church in Aswan.
>
> Around 7:30 PM, I received text and Twitter messages that an announcer for State TV had on air called for Egyptians to go down and "defend the soldiers who protected the Egyptian revolution" against "armed Copts" who had opened fire and were killing soldiers. Looking around me, I could see that many of those gathered in the tight area around the TV building seemed to have responded to the call. Rough-looking men were arriving in groups; people said they were neighborhood thugs. They held bludgeons, wooden planks, knives, and even swords, and walked boldly into the chaos of burning cars, flying bullets, and glass. "We'll kill any Christian we get our hands on," one of them

shouted. Someone tweeted that he was in the middle of what looked like a militia, "men with clubs and antique pistols." Nearby, a young girl was harassed, and a mob assaulted a young Coptic couple, beating them and ripping their clothes. One of the perpetrators emerged from the gang with blood on his hands. "Christian blood!" he boasted. (The couple survived – rushed away by ambulance to be treated for wounds and possible fractures.)[6]

Once again the traditional scapegoat had been found. It was once the Jews, but for decades had been the Christians. Subsequent marches to remember the slaughtered Christians and the smashed churches were themselves attacked by Muslim mobs, and in November in Ghorayzat two Christian brothers were murdered as Muslim gangs ran through the Christian district attacking bystanders and smashing property. The year ended with five Christians being attacked in Assiut after an allegedly offensive cartoon had appeared on Facebook.

In January 2012 in Kebly-Rahmaniya, a man and a young boy were shot as a Muslim mob rampaged through the town attacking Christians and Christian homes; in Bangourah, a Christian father and son were shot to death by a Muslim gang. In Abu Al-Reesh in March, two nuns were hurt when fifteen hundred Muslims besieged a Catholic school, once again after rumours that a new church was to be built, and in July in Shubra el Khayma, a Christian doctor was tortured and then blinded by Salafists after he asked them to stop shooting their weapons at a celebration because he was worried that they as well as other people would be hurt by falling bullets. As the year came to a close, two Christians were shot in their home by Muslim intruders in Abdelmassih; the intruders had been trying to kidnap and convert a twenty-four-year-old member of the family.

In February 2013 in Alexandria, a Christian woman was stabbed as she walked along the middle of a street, and in the same month in the same city four Christians and a Muslim guard were killed outside their church. In March in Cairo, another church-building rumour began to spread, almost certainly false and part of a concerted campaign of provocation, leading to the shooting deaths of three Christians. A week later, terrorists linked to the Muslim Brotherhood, who have claimed to oppose anti-Christian violence, attacked a group of Christian worshippers; in July in Cairo, a group of Christians leaving their church after a funeral were attacked, one person being killed during the first attack and another shortly afterwards. In Khusus, a twenty-six-year-old Christian was covered with gasoline and set on fire, in Alexandria a Copt was murdered during a church attack, in Cairo a six-year-old Christian boy was kidnapped by a Muslim gang and later killed, and in Nagaa Hassan four Christians were hacked to death by supporters of the Muslim Brotherhood. In the summer, a ten-year-old girl in Ain Shams was shot dead outside her church, and in Souhag a Christian store was attacked and those inside murdered. In August in Alexandria, a Christian taxi driver was dragged screaming from his vehicle and decapitated, in Minya two Christians were killed and many others injured when churches were attacked, and in the same town and in the same month two guards on a boat owned by a Christian were killed. In September, two Christians were shot dead in Sahel Selim for refusing to pay the religious tax, the *jizya*, to Muslims, in October a sixty-year-old Christian man was killed defending his wife from a Muslim mob in Dalga, and in October in Warraq, a church minister, a woman, and two young girls were shot dead inside their church. The year ended with a virtual pogrom in Minya.

In February 2014, a bus full of Christian tourists from South Korea was bombed by the Sinai-based jihadist group Ansar Bait al-Maqdis. Three Koreans and the Egyptian driver were killed and seventeen people were badly injured. They had just left Saint Catherine's Monastery in the Sinai and were about to cross into Israel to visit Christian pilgrimage sites there. Devout Presbyterians, they had reportedly saved for years to visit biblical sites on the sixtieth anniversary of their church.

The Rev. Majed El Shafie is a human rights advocate and founder of One Free World International. Born a Muslim in Egypt, he converted to Christianity and shortly afterwards was arrested, tortured, and sentenced to death. His conversion was particularly irksome to radical Muslims because he came from a highly respected Muslim family well known in the country's legal and political community. He managed to escape but was forced to flee the country and now travels the world speaking for persecuted minorities and particularly for Christians living under Islamic rule.

"There are degrees of persecution," he explains. "It starts with the basic fact that Christians are treated as second-class citizens. There is official and unofficial discrimination on many levels, from not being able to build churches to the police turning a blind eye to minor and even major crimes against Christians. Then there is the inability of converts to register as Christians. It seems like an unimportant matter to us in the West but when your religion is required on government-issued identity documents and determines everything (officially or unofficially) from whom you can and cannot marry to inheritance matters, it is a matter of critical importance to people's daily lives. But this is an inconvenience compared to the death threats and physical attacks converts receive – often from their own family-members – which frequently force them into hiding. Christians by family history, on the other hand, can live their second-class existence in relative peace but with the constant fear that they or their family-members might be targeted for physical attacks and attempts at forced conversion, or rape as punishment in response to the smallest indiscretion or for no reason at all other than their faith.

"The Muslim Brotherhood wants to institutionalize this persecution by focusing on developing Shariah law as the law of the land. On the other hand, with General Sisi there is the fear that the country is going back to the Mubarak system where the state controls everything with an iron fist and sacrifices the minorities in order to keep Muslim extremists in check. Christianity spread rapidly to Egypt and in the first few centuries after Christ it was a primarily Christian country. When Islam came to Egypt at the edge of the sword in the 7th century, things changed drastically. Since then the persecution has never stopped; it has just changed in form and degree from time to time, but it has always been there."[7]

The underlying question is whether the persecution of Christians by Muslims is a modern aberration, an abuse of the Koran, a misunderstanding of the teachings of Mohammad, or something intrinsic and integral to the Muslim faith. In other words, are moderate Muslims the true believers or is it the fundamentalists who have properly understood the message correctly?

El Shafie believes, "It is a combination of both. It is in the religion itself, if you look at surah 5 verses 57 and 60, also surah 5:51, and surah 9:29, where clearly the Koran speaks against the

'People of the Book,' meaning Christians and Jews. However, that doesn't mean that all Muslims will go around killing Christians. What we are really seeing right now is that if you are more committed to the religion you will be more likely to follow the precepts of the Koran to the letter. But if you are a 'moderate' or 'secular' Muslim, your attitude and actions may range from a measure of tolerance toward non-Muslims to a degree of generalized bigotry and intolerance. This can be seen everywhere in the attitudes of people in the street and the broader mentality of the culture in Muslim countries. In parts of Egypt and Pakistan, for example, if a Christian drinks from a Muslim's glass, the Muslim will break the glass because the Christian is considered 'dirty' and the glass can therefore no longer be used by a Muslim. The main dilemma facing Islam as a faith today is not the rising of Islamic extremism but the silence of the moderate Muslims which makes them a partner in the crimes of the extremists."

Father Zakaria Boutros, whom we mentioned in the introduction, is convinced that it's theology more than application that is the problem. "We can ask Islam to adapt to modernity, we can demand that it respects human rights and modern values, we can seduce it with the temptations of the west and of liberalism, but these will only work in the short term. Turkey moderated for a while, even my own Egypt changed under the influence of a nationalist leader like Nasser and when we were told that the common enemy was Israel, but all of this was mere window dressing. Islam always re-emerges through the cracks that will always emerge. We're speaking here of a religion, a legal system, and an ideology that through military power began as a small cavalry army in the desert and managed to conquer half the world and indeed remain in control of that half of the world. Remember, the situation is not getting any better but only getting worse."

Egypt is the Christian key in the door to the Arab world. There will always be Christians in the country, but if the exile continues and the persecution does not stop – and it shows absolutely no signs of doing so – numbers will reduce and begin to resemble those of other Arab countries, and Christianity will become little more than a humiliating minority having no impact or influence on the most powerful country in the Arab world. If Egyptian Christianity drains to a trickle, the Christians of the rest of the Middle East will become virtually invisible. The purging will have been complete.

PAKISTAN

THE PLACE OF CHRISTIANS in Pakistan is a unique one, different in history and context from the followers of Christ in the Middle East whom we have discussed earlier. Christians form the second-largest minority after Hinduism in this Islamic nation, one that was specifically created for the Muslims of the Indian subcontinent. There are around 2.5 million Christians in Pakistan, divided fairly evenly between Catholicism and various Protestant denominations. Many of them, from both parts of the Christian faith, trace their faith back not to ancient times or the Catholic expansionism of the sixteenth century but to British imperial rule in the eighteenth, nineteenth, and early twentieth centuries. Pakistan came into being 1947, and the Christian community in the region had been far from opposed to the creation of a separate Muslim nation independent of overwhelmingly Hindu India. Muhammad Ali Jinnah, effectively the founder of Pakistan, was a cultured and civilized man who saw his infant state as a nation for Muslims rather than as a Muslim nation, and he welcomed non-Muslims and especially Christians as full citizens. Tragically, the country changed direction quite radically after Jinnah's death, becoming an Islamic Republic in 1956 and enshrining the Islamic faith as the essence of Pakistani citizenship, culture, and being. Large numbers of Hindus, Sikhs, and Christians left Pakistan in the 1960s and 1970s but matters have become far worse for those Christians who have stayed in the country. In the past thirty years, with the rigid application of the country's draconian blasphemy laws (which will be discussed later), an increasing Islamic radicalization, and a suspicion of all things non-Muslim, Christians in Pakistan have lived tenuous and dangerous lives.

Tarek Fatah is a Pakistani-born Muslim author and journalist who now lives in Canada and writes frequently about Islam's persecution of minorities. "It is pretty awful if one is an indigenous Christian in Pakistan today, which in most cases are the Punjabi-speaking Christians whose forefathers converted mostly from the low-caste Hindus to Christianity in the 19th century at the hands of English missionaries. It will not be an exaggeration to say they live lives of near apartheid in their own separate communities, and [are] considered 'unclean' by their Muslim neighbours. It is quite common in Pakistan to see well-meaning middle class Muslim families keep separate utensils and crockery for Christian working class, often their domestic help. The discrimination is NOT because they are Christians, but is compounded because they are dark-skinned and working class. I say this because the same Pakistani Muslim who would not share his or her table with a Pakistani Punjabi Christian would have no problem hosting a European or American White Christian.

"At [Pakistan's] inception in 1947, Pakistani Christians could be divided in three categories. a) Punjabi rural working class Anglicans, b) Catholic urban middle class Goans in Karachi, and c) White Anglo-Indians who lived in Karachi, Lahore, Rawalpindi and Quetta and this included both Irish Catholic and English Protestants. The latter two groups were largely English-speaking and were in the middle to upper middle class presence right up to the early 1960s. The Punjabi Anglicans were even then on the sidelines, but in a more secular environment, their lives and property were never in danger and they escaped the horrendous bloodshed that took place during Partition. Christians were the only community that escaped mass slaughter between Sikhs and Muslims. As late as 1958, Pakistan's Test Cricket team had such names as wicket keeper Duncan Sharpe (Anglo-Indian), Wallis Mathias (slip fielder and No. 3 bat) and Antao D'Souza (medium pacer) and no one felt they were out of place. Antao and Wallis were Goans. By [the] late 1950s, most of the Anglo-Indians [had] left for Australia and the Goans slowly started to trickle towards Canada, Australia and the US and today there are no Anglo-Indians and few Goans left. Only the Punjabi dark-skinned Anglicans are left behind to face the monstrosities of Islamism."[1]

The story of persecution and barbarism in the past fourteen years makes for distressing reading. In 2001 in Bahawalpur, six Islamic fundamentalists attacked a church with automatic weapons and killed seventeen Christians, five of them children. Nine other worshippers were badly injured. The following year, 2002, began just as badly when in Islamabad Islamists threw hand grenades into a church and killed five Christians and injured another forty-five. A few months later in Kachi Abadi, a fifteen-year-old was killed by the police for blaspheming Islam and the prophet Mohammad; in the same area a seventeen-year-old Christian woman was blinded after acid was thrown into her face. A few days later, another Christian girl was assaulted, beaten, and raped. In Faisalabad, a teenaged girl was attacked with acid – a now common form of assault – for refusing to convert from Christianity to Islam, and in August in Jhika Gali, six people were killed and another four injured when Islamists attacked a Christian school. The following month in Karachi, seven Christians were blindfolded, tied up, and shot through the head. The year ended with the murder of three women in a Daska church. Fourteen other women were badly injured.

In 2003 in Ranala Kot, a Catholic priest was murdered in his home by an Islamic gang, a year later in Khanewai another priest was assassinated as he waited for a train, and in Karachi a dozen people were injured in a bomb explosion at a Christian Bible Society office. In April 2014 in Lahore, a Christian pastor was shot dead by a Muslim assassin, and the following month in Toba Tek Singh, a Catholic student was kidnapped, tortured, and killed when he refused to embrace Islam; a week later in Karachi, four Christians were killed on their way to a picnic. At the end of the month in Lahore, a Christian was attacked with a hammer by a police officer for allegedly transgressing Pakistan's blasphemy laws. The victim later died and the policeman boasted that he had now earned a "spot in Paradise." In August in Lahore, a twenty-six-year-old Christian was dragged from his home and murdered, and in October in Karachi, six workers in a Christian charity store were shot in the back of the head and killed.

In March 2005 in Khambay, an Easter service was attacked by an Islamist gang, with one man being killed and six others injured. In August in Lahore, a Catholic man was abducted, tortured, and killed and another member of the same Catholic community was kidnapped and strangled to death. At the end of the year in Rawalpindi, a twenty-three-year-old Christian and his Muslim girlfriend were murdered by Islamists because of their relationship. In 2006 in Bahawlnager, a Christian man was arrested, imprisoned, and killed for blaspheming the Muslim faith, and a Christian missionary was shot dead in Azad Kashmir. In 2007 in Islamabad, a Christian man was murdered in the street by jihadists, and in January 2008 in Sheikhupura, a thirteen-year-old boy was murdered by Islamic radicals. This was followed in the Punjab by the kidnapping of a sixteen-year-old Christian, whose organs were then sold, and in Peshawar by the murder a month later of two Christians. In May in Hafizabad, a nineteen-year-old boy was tortured and killed for dating a Muslim girl, and in Lahore, another Christian was abducted, tortured, and killed for the same "crime."[2]

In February 2009, a Christian man who had been denied his wages was killed by his employers, and the following month in Songo, a Muslim mob stormed a Presbyterian church and clubbed a forty-five-year-old woman to death. In April in Taseer, two Christians were killed and another injured when a gang of Islamists entered the Christian district in large numbers and armed, and in May in Machharkay, a Christian was murdered because he drank tea at a "Muslim only" café. In the same month in Punjab, a Christian man was sodomized and murdered for refusing to convert, and in Tiasar an eleven-year-old boy was shot by the Taliban inside his church. In June in Bahawalpur, ten Christians were badly injured when a parcel bomb exploded in their community centre, and in the same month in Ittanwali, two small children were beaten after their mother refused to give in to an Islamic gang's demands and convert to the Muslim faith. In July, there were four major attacks. In Faisalabad, a Christian youth was tortured by Muslims after being accused of defacing a copy of the Koran; in Lahore, fifteen Christian women were badly burned when acid was thrown at them, and a Christian was shot eight times in the legs and crippled for life after he refused to pay the Islamic tax on Christians, the *jizya*; in Ghaziabad, a sixteen-year-old Christian boy was murdered in a police station. In August in

Gorja, a Christian was killed after being beaten by a Muslim mob, and in the same city seven Christians, including a four-year-old child, were burned to death when mobs invaded the Christian area to conduct what was in effect an anti-Christian pogrom. In Quetta in August, six Christians were murdered after refusing to convert, and the following month in Sialkot, a young Christian man was beaten to death for the crime of blasphemy. December and the approach of Christmas was especially bloody. In Karol, a Christian was shot dead for refusing to convert, in Punjab two Christians were shot dead for the same crime, and in Kalar Kahar more than fifty Christians were injured when a church was attacked. The year ended in Peshawar with a suicide bomber blowing himself up close to a Christian school and killing four people.

In 2010 in Lahore, a twelve-year-old Christian girl was raped and murdered by her Muslim employer, and in Punjab, a Christian man was beaten to death for refusing to convert to Islam. In Karachi in February, a Christian family was wiped out by two bombs, one placed at a hospital, and the following month in Lahore a man was shot dead by Islamist gunmen. In March in Oghi, six Christian charity workers were forced at gunpoint from their office and shot to death in the street, and in the same month in Rawalpindi, a Christian woman was raped and her husband burned to death after he refused to become a Muslim. In April in Punjab, ten Christians were beaten senseless by a Muslim mob, and in Sargodha a Christian barber was sodomized and beaten for cutting the beard of a Muslim man after the customer had specifically requested that his beard be cut. Also in April in Karachi, a Christian policeman was abducted and tortured to death, and in Sargodha two Christian teenagers were beaten and hospitalized by an Islamic mob. One of the boys succumbed to his wounds.

The year 2005 was no better. In Faisalabad in May, a Muslim gang opened fire on a crowd of Christian worshippers, injuring five of them, and the following month in Sahiwal, a Christian minister and his heavily pregnant wife were beaten up by a Muslim mob after being accused of trying to convert Muslims to Christianity. Also in June in Punjab, a gang led by Islamic clerics smashed their way into a private home and murdered a Christian woman and her four children, and in Peshawar a Christian teacher at a college was beaten up by his own students when he argued with them about religion and refused to become a Muslim. In July in Sukkur, five Christians were murdered outside of their church, one of the five being the church's minister. July was particularly brutal: in Karachi, a Christian was raped and then thrown to her death by a Muslim doctor; in Faisalabad, two Christian brothers who were also ordained ministers were standing trial for blasphemy and were shot dead outside the court in which they were being tried; finally, in Rawalpindi, two Christians girls, both of them virgins, were gang-raped by a large group of Muslims.

In August in Swat, three Christian charity workers helping both Muslim and Christian victims of the recent and deadly flooding in the region were murdered by Islamists, and in October in Haripur, an entire family was murdered. World Watch Monitor reported that "Islamic extremists killed a Christian lawyer, his wife and their five children in northwestern Pakistan this week for mounting a legal challenge against a Muslim who was charging a Christian exorbitant interest, local sources said.

"Police found the bodies of attorney and evangelist Edwin Paul and his family on Tuesday morning (Sept. 28) at their home in Haripur, a small town near Abbotabad in Khyber Pakhtunkhwa Province (previously known as the North-West Frontier Province, or NWFP), according to Haripur Station House Officer (SHO) Maqbool Khan.

"The victim and his wife Ruby Paul, along with their five children ages 6 to 17, had been shot to death.

"'On Sept. 28 at around 8 a.m., we received a call from Sher Khan colony that people heard gunshots, and there was a group of people who ran from a house and drove away,' Khan said. 'We went and found seven bodies in a house.'

"Paul's Muslim neighbor, Mushtaq Khan, [said] that the previous day a group of armed men had threatened the lawyer.

"'On Monday a group of armed men stopped Paul and took him by the collar and said, 'Leave the town in 24 hours – we know how to throw out Christians, we will not allow even a single Christian to live here. We will hang them all in the streets, so that no Christian would ever dare to enter the Hazara land.'"[3]

Age does not seem to be an issue. In August in Punjab, an octogenarian couple was beaten into unconsciousness by a Muslim gang. In November in Sargodha, a minister was beaten up and set ablaze by a mob, then at the beginning of 2011 in Shahdra in a most repugnant case, a twelve-year-old girl was abducted, held hostage for more than eight months, repeatedly beaten and raped, and forced to convert to Islam. The year became central in the evolution of anti-Christian violence. At the beginning of January, the governor of Punjab, Salman Taseer, was assassinated by one of his security guards. Voice of America (VOA) reported:

Pakistani Interior Minister Rehman Malik says the slain governor . . . was returning to his car after visiting a shopping center in the Pakistani capital when one of his armed guards sprayed him with bullets.

Witnesses say the Punjab Governor fell down and the attacker dropped his gun before surrendering to police.

Interior Minister Malik told reporters an investigation has been ordered into the incident.

The minister says the assassin told investigators he killed the Punjab governor because of Taseer's opposition to Pakistan's controversial Islamic law of blasphemy.

Governor Taseer was making efforts to secure the release of a Christian woman sentenced to death by a court for making derogatory remarks against the Prophet Mohammad.

Taseer's actions along with recent demands by human-rights groups to reform the Islamic law to prevent its misuse have angered religious parties in the country. Islamic groups have also staged street protests in recent days to warn the government against amending the law.

Federal Minister for Minorities Shahbaz Bhatti, while speaking to VOA, condemned the killing as a barbaric act. He defended the slain Punjab governor for speaking against the misuse of the Islamic law of blasphemy.

"This cowardly act of violence cannot stop people who believe that this law (blasphemy law) is being misused as a tool to victimize the innocent people of Pakistan," Bhatti said. "And I ask the government and other law enforcement agencies to investigate all those who instigated the people and issued the decrees against the governor."[4]

The intensity of violence did not stop there. Shahbaz Bhatti, who is quoted in the article above, was the single

Christian minister in the Pakistani government, and I interviewed him shortly after the murder of his friend Salman Taseer. He was fully aware of the threats against him and the dangers of being such a prominent Christian in modern Pakistan but he was determined to continue to represent his people and what he insisted was the true essence of Pakistan. "I do not believe, I cannot allow myself to believe, that fundamentalism and extremism is the future of this country, of my country," he said. "The problem, of course, is that what was once a fringe is now much of the centre. Pakistan always enjoyed a large and powerful establishment that looked to Western and secular values and could resist rural radicalism. Sometimes the violence is so repetitive and so deep that it hardly registers. Then I see the faces of the shot, the beaten, the stabbed, the raped, and the dead. I have to fight on. I think we still can win but, in all honesty, sometimes I am not sure. But I hope, I hope, I live in hope."[5]

Tragically, hope was insufficient. In March, he was murdered by assassins reportedly sent by al-Qaeda and the Taliban. Only forty-two years old, a faithful Roman Catholic, and a proud Pakistani, he was killed in the heart of the country's capital. He was driving from his mother's Islamabad home. The *Daily Mail* in Britain reported: "Mr Bhatti had defied warnings after receiving death threats for urging reform of the laws and his death further undermines Pakistan's shaky image as a moderate Islamic state – deepening the political turmoil in this nuclear-armed, U.S.-allied state where militants frequently stage suicide attacks.

"A branch of the Taliban claimed responsibility for the death of what they called a 'blasphemer' and warned: 'We will continue to target all those who speak against the law which punishes those who insult the prophet. Their fate will be the same.' . . .

"Mr Bhatti said he was threatened by the Taliban and Al Qaeda, but that this would not deter him from speaking for 'oppressed and marginalized persecuted Christians and other minorities' in Pakistan.

"'I will die to defend their rights,' he said. 'These threats and these warnings cannot change my opinions and principles.'

"Despite the threats, Mr Bhatti, who had been assigned bodyguards, was without protection. The politician had just pulled out of the driveway of the house, where he frequently stayed, when three men standing nearby opened fire, said Gulam Rahim, a witness.

"Two of the men opened the door of the car and tried to pull Mr Bhatti out," Rahim said, while a third man fired his Kalashnikov rifle repeatedly into the dark-colored Toyota, shattering the windows.

"The gunmen then sped away in a white Suzuki Mehran car, said Rahim who took shelter behind a tree. Bhatti was dead on arrival at an area hospital, while his driver was not harmed.

"Government officials condemned the killing, but made no reference to the blasphemy law controversy which has been in the international spotlight since a Christian woman was sentenced to die last November for allegedly insulting the Prophet Mohammad during a row with Muslim women. She denies the claims.

"Mr Bhatti, who was minister for religious minorities, had been given police and paramilitary guards, but rarely used them because it had been a bodyguard who in January had killed killed Punjab province Governor Salman Taseer, another opponent of the blasphemy laws.

"To the horror of Pakistan's besieged liberals, many ordinary citizens praised the governor's assassin – a sign of the spread of hardline Islamist thought in the country.

"Mr Bhatti had requested a bullet-proof car but had not been given one."[6]

The woman sentenced to death for blasphemy was Aasiya Noreen, generally known as Asia Bibi, who at the time of writing has just had her appeal hearing postponed for the third time. She was initially charged in November 2009 after an argument with her colleagues and has spent the years since in prison. The original argument was over the fact that she drank water from the same bottle as her Muslim co-workers while they were all harvesting berries. They claimed she blasphemed against Mohammad during the argument, but she denied the claim. It's a case of Alice in Wonderland proportions, in that whether the poor woman blasphemed or not is or should be irrelevant. It's likely, however, that as with so many such accusations the motives were personal and the victim never even mentioned religion. She is illiterate, poor, and vulnerable, but with the help of a translator she has managed to have a memoir published. It's as compelling as is it heart-breaking:

"At that moment, I was hit in the face. My nose is hurting. I am bleeding. I am half stunned. They pull me as though I were a stubborn donkey. I can do nothing other than suffer and pray that it stops. I look at the crowd, which seems to triumph at my feeble resistance. I stagger. The blows fall on to my legs, on to my back, behind my head. 'Do you want to convert, to belong to a religion worthy of the name?' No, please, I am a Christian. I beg you. And with the same fury, they continue to beat me. One arm is really hurting. I think it may be broken. 'Death to the Christian!' the angry mob scream, and I cried alone, putting my head in my hands. I can no longer bear the sight of people full of hatred, applauding the killing of a poor farm worker. I no longer see them, but I still hear them, the crowd who gave the judge a standing ovation, saying: 'Kill her, kill her! Allahu akbar!' The courthouse is invaded by a euphoric horde who break down the doors, chanting: 'Vengeance for the holy prophet. Allah is great!' I was then thrown like an old rubbish sack into the van. . . . I had lost all humanity in their eyes."

In spite of enormous international pressure, the case continues and all notions of international law are ignored. But that comes as no surprise to Pakistan's Christians. The violence and the hatred grind on day by day and year by year. In March 2011 in Hyderabad, two Christians were killed outside their church, and in the same city in the same month, a Pentecostal church was attacked by a Muslim mob that destroyed property, smashed crosses, ripped up Bibles, and killed two people. In April in Gujranwala, there was a series of attacks: first, a dozen Christians were dragged from their church and beaten; then more than three hundred Muslims invaded a church and assaulted Christians; then another church was attacked and Christians beaten, robbed, and chased out of the town. In Hamza, a Christian minister was attacked, his son beaten into unconsciousness, and a Christian woman raped. In July in Farmwala, a little boy was beaten for refusing to convert to Islam; in Landhi, a Christian was shot dead; and in Lahore, a Christian father of four children was stabbed to death. The victim had worked as a garbage collector; Christians in Pakistan are routinely relegated to jobs that Muslims refuse to perform. As 2011 progressed, the attacks became more blatant and organized. In August in Karachi, two Christians were attacked with iron bars, and in Bilal a group of Catholics were beaten up; in the same month in Faisalabad, a sixty-four-year-old man was mobbed by a large group of madrassah students after he had held a Christian Bible reading and prayer service in his home. In September in Mariamabad, a Catholic was killed while making a pilgrimage to a shrine. In the same month in Islamabad, a Christian died in prison after being arrested for blasphemy; he had allegedly been denied medical treatment even though he had repeatedly requested it and was in obvious distress. Then in Lahore, a teenaged girl was murdered by her uncle after she had dated a Christian boy.

In October in Milan Channu, a Christian was killed after trying to build an orphanage for a church, and in Korangi, a Christian woman's throat was cut after she had been raped. In November in Abbottabad, a Christian woman who was heavily pregnant was tortured and beaten by the police for several hours, and in the same month in Karachi, a minister was shot in the head. Also in November in Khurda Renala, a Catholic man was shot dead; in Muzaffargarh, two Christian women were attacked by a Muslim gang; and in December, a Christian was stabbed several times by Muslims in Lahore after being accused of blasphemy. In Plateau, three Christians, including a baby, were hacked to death. The year 2012 began with an attack in Kot Meerath when a Christian woman was first tortured and then dragged through the streets with signs around her neck explaining that she had insulted Islam and Mohammad. In May in Dhamala, three Christian women were attacked and beaten in a private home, and in Quetta, a Christian man was killed while leaving work. In July in Kot Ghulam, a Christian was stopped while driving in his truck, asked his religion, and then dragged from the cab and shot dead. In the same month in Hyderabad, two Christians were murdered by a Muslim gang.

In August in Karachi, a worshipper was killed and his pastor badly injured in a gun attack, and in Faisalabad, a fourteen-year-old Christian boy was tortured and killed. In September in Mardan, a Lutheran church was firebombed, in Hyderabad a nun and her driver were killed outside of a cathedral they were visiting, and in Karachi a mass attack led to the deaths of two Christians. The year ended with violence in Iqbal against Christian families, and in Ittehad Chowk, one man was killed and another shot.

In January 2013 in Bahawalpur, a Christian was stabbed to death for dating a Muslim girl, and in February in Chaman, a Christian was shot five times and killed when he refused to convert. Three Christian women in Pattoki were beaten by a mob in their homes, and in Lahore a middle-aged Christian man was killed by Muslims after a conversation about religion. In March in Lahore, a pogrom took place when mobs of Muslims stormed through a Christian area, burning dozens of homes and injuring a number of people. In April in Gujranwala, eighteen Christians were beaten by Muslim gangs after a particularly aggressive sermon at a local mosque, and in the same month in Manga Mandi, a young Christian man was shot through the head. In Manghopir, two guards outside a Belgian missionary school were shot dead. In May in Karachi, a Christian was shot dead as he walked home, and in Khushpur a teenager was killed when a Christian village was burned to the ground by Islamists. In the summer in Sheikhupura, a Christian boy was killed after being accused of seeing a Muslim girl, in Islamabad one person was killed when a church was attacked, and in Okara a Christian was executed in front of his family. Then the Peshawar massacre occurred. The *New York Times* reported:

"A suicide attack on a historic church in northwestern Pakistan killed at least 78 people on Sunday in one of the deadliest attacks on the Christian minority in Pakistan in years.

"The attack occurred as worshipers left All Saints Church in the old quarter of the regional capital, Peshawar, after a service on Sunday morning. Up to 600 people had attended and were leaving to receive free food being distributed on the lawn outside when two explosions ripped through the crowd. 'As soon as the service finished and the food was being distributed, all of a sudden we heard one explosion, followed by another,' said Azim Ghori, a witness.

"Interior Minister Chaudhry Nisar Ali Khan, who arrived in Peshawar on Sunday evening, said that 78 people had been killed, including 34 women and 7 children. Akhtar Ali Shah, the home secretary of Khyber Pakhtunkhwa Province, said that more than 100 people had been wounded. Mr. Khan said that 37 of those were children. . . .

"Witnesses reported scenes of mayhem as rescue workers ferried victims from the church, which was scattered with body parts, shrapnel and bloodied clothing.

"On Sunday afternoon, the bodies of 45 victims were placed in coffins and moved to the nearby St. John's Church, the oldest church in the city. The coffins were placed in the church playground as dozens of grieving relatives and mourners gathered. A large contingent of police officers was deployed outside the church, and mourners were allowed to enter the compound after a thorough security check. Ambulances were allowed to enter the compound one by one as dead bodies were then placed in vehicles to take them to the morgue. . . .

"All Saints Church is one of the oldest in Peshawar and was built during the British colonial era. It is at Kohati Gate in the city's old quarter, where numerous militant attacks have occurred in recent years, mostly targeting Muslims."[7]

The numbers were greater than usual but the spirit and the hatred and the malice were nothing new. The year 2013 ended with an attack in Karachi when two Christians and their uncle were beaten in their homes for refusing to convert to Islam, and in Islamabad in December, a Christian man was arrested and tortured to death by Islamist police officers. In the year of writing, 2014, the situation was just as bad and there was no indication that matters would improve.

Farzana Hassan is a highly respected author, journalist, and activist who has written and broadcast widely on issues of Islam, persecution, and the plight of minorities under Muslim rule. Although a Muslim, she received her early education in Lahore at the Sacred Heart Catholic School, before studying in North America. She has headed the Muslim Canadian Congress, and the Canadian Muslim National Christian Liaison Committee gave her their annual service award in 2004.

She says, "9/11 seems to have fanned the already simmering hostility towards Christians in Pakistan. Christians have always been a shunned and beleaguered community since the country came into existence in 1947. They mostly work as menials and laborers. As a result they occupy the lowest rung of the social ladder. However, the killings and church burnings, blasphemy laws, and the witch hunts that many Christians face today appear to be a recent phenomenon sparked by the 9/11 tragedy and the growth of militant groups in Pakistan. Christians are blamed as fifth columnists, more in cahoots with the great Satan, the United States and its allies in the West.

"I visited Pakistan in 2013 and spoke to a number of people about some recent assaults on Christians in the country.

Whereas hostility towards Christians seems to be less acute among the upper, educated classes, lower middle middle-class people seem to think that Christians themselves actually provoke the attacks. The lower classes constitute 80 per cent of Pakistan's population, therefore the hostility, even if it does not always translate into violence, is still quite widespread. In the sixties and seventies there was more of a 'live and let live' policy towards minority religious communities except perhaps the Ahmediayya. But the blasphemy laws enacted by the dictator Ziaul Haqq have rendered Christians vulnerable to persecution also involving charges of blasphemy. They can be castigated for the slightest perceived provocation. The examples of Asia Bib and Rimsha Masih come to mind immediately."[8]

We discussed Asia Bib earlier but Rimsha Masih is another case that needs to be more widely exposed. Masih was arrested in August 2012 in Islamabad after a Muslim cleric accused her of burning a copy of the Koran. She was thought to be eleven years old, but there are disputes about her age and she could have been thirteen or fourteen. There is also conflicting evidence as to her mental state, with some reports claiming that she has a mental disability or perhaps Down's syndrome. Either way, she is a child. She was held in prison until released on bail, and her accuser was subsequently accused of fabricating evidence. Partly because of this and also due to massive international condemnation, the case was eventually dropped. There were fears, however, that she was even more at risk outside of prison than under police incarceration, as many people, even those charged with blasphemy, whatever their age or gender, are highly likely to be victims of vigilante justice and murdered by Islamic mobs. The lawyer representing Masih, Rao Abdur Raheem, pleaded with the courts to give his client special protection as "Muslims could take the law into their own hands." She later fled to Canada for protection.

Peter Bhatti is chairman of International Christian Voice and lives in Canada and says of Masih, "She is safe now, and is doing very well, but she still receives death threats and her extended family back in Pakistan are still frightened of what might happen after two years. The point, though, is that she was one of the lucky ones. Most people accused of blasphemy are not as young and don't pull on international heartstrings. They are arrested, beaten, tortured, and if released often killed by Muslims who think the blasphemy laws are not strict enough. Nor can we comfort ourselves by thinking that the laws have limited support in Pakistan. They have enormous support, and to oppose is – as we know – extremely dangerous."

In March 2014, a court sentenced Sàwan Masih to death for blasphemy over an incident that triggered a riot in the country's second-largest city. The name Masih, or Messiah, is common among Pakistani Christians and Sawan is not related to Rimsha. He was convicted of insulting the prophet Mohammad during a conversation with a Muslim friend in the Joseph Colony neighbourhood of Lahore in 2013. Raheel Raza is a Pakistani Muslim writer, activist, and author who has spoken out bravely and often about the plight of Christians and increasing extremism of other Pakistani Muslims. "There are various issues that create problems. The Blasphemy Law allows anyone who has a grudge to victimize a non-Muslim. Once this happens there is no stopping the mob frenzy. Pakistani law mandates that any 'blasphemies' of the Quran are to be met with punishment. On July 28, 1994, Amnesty International urged Pakistan's late Prime Minister, Benazir Bhutto to change the law because it was being used to terrorize religious minorities.

She tried but was unsuccessful. However, she modified the laws to make them more moderate. Her changes were reversed by the Nawaz Sharif administration. Therefore Christians don't find justice in Pakistan. It wasn't always this way. When Pakistan was created as an independent country in 1947, the founder of Pakistan Mohammad Ali Jinnah spoke eloquently about the rights of minorities in Pakistan and indicated that the white portion of the Pakistan flag represents minorities.

"I lived in Pakistan till the 1970's and went to a Convent school run by Catholic nuns – so obviously it couldn't be as bad as it is now.

"Christians have been part of major institutions in Pakistan like nursing, schools and administrative roles including largely in the banking and travel industry. In the late 1970's Pakistan's then President General Zia ul Haq, influenced by Saudi Arabia, started dividing people along lines of faith and religious denominations. So even Muslim minorities were singled out as being on the fringe. However Pakistani Christians, who are largely peace-loving and mild people, received the brunt of the backlash."[9]

"In the 1990s, some Christians were arrested on charges of blasphemy, and for what appeared to be an insult to Islam. John Joseph, a bishop in Faisalabad committed suicide to protest the execution of a Christian man on blasphemy charges. Some people accused of blasphemy have been killed in prison or shot dead in court, and even if pardoned, may remain in danger from imams in their local village. Ayub Masih, a Christian, was convicted of blasphemy and sentenced to death in 1998. He was accused by a neighbor of stating that he supported British writer, Salman Rushdie, author of *The Satanic Verses*. In September 2013, 85 people were killed and more than

100 injured when Taliban bombed the All Saints' church in Peshawar. Apart from this there are reports of Christian villages being burnt, Christian women being forced to convert to Islam and personal vendettas being settled through accusations of blasphemy."[10]

The fundamental question, however, is whether this current terror is intrinsic to Islam or somehow a product of a modern and passing anger. It's the same question that applies to Islamic intolerance of Christians and Christianity throughout the world. "I believe that it's Islam as practiced today which we call political Islam or Islamism," says Raza. "There is no debate/ discussion on this issue and no answers – ever. If we focus on Islamic injunctions taken out of context, then we can't blame the whole religion as we won't find solutions. This is a human rights travesty. Every faith has had violence issues i.e. witches being burned at the stake but [we] can't blame all of Christianity for this because they saw the problem and eliminated it from their faith. Similarly in Hinduism widows were burnt as the practice of Sati – however that too has been made illegal. We still have to make persecution of Christians in Pakistan a criminal offence with accountability. Unfortunately Pakistani Christians have not put forward a forceful case. At the UN Human Rights Council, other persecuted communities come in hordes to present their case like the Ahamddiya and Bahai, but not Pakistani Christians. When they come to the West, one would hope that they liaise with mainstream Churches, but they have their own Churches. They also have a passionate love for Pakistan so it's sort of like the Stockholm syndrome."

But Pakistan is a nuclear power, it supports or at least pretends to support Western policies in Afghanistan, and without Pakistani cooperation or lack of opposition, the war on terror led by the United States would be severely diminished. Frankly, very few Western politicians care very much about Pakistan's Christians and none seem prepared to risk their relationships with Pakistan by championing this besieged minority. Pakistan is in genuine danger, and a successful Islamist revolution is not out of the question. The security and intelligence services, highly sympathetic to and infiltrated by Muslim radicals, is dominant, the liberal intelligentsia is limping and weak, and Pakistan's sense of paranoia and inadequacy when juxtaposed with neighbouring India grows ever stronger. Pakistan's Christians have never been so vulnerable and so alone.

IRAN

IRAN IS THE ONLY MAJOR Shi'ite Muslim power in the world, and while the current regime boasts of a universal Islamic brotherhood, the Iranian people generally feel superior to Arabs and central Asian Muslims and are deeply suspicious of Turks. Still, this doesn't prevent them from sharing with those peoples a dislike for and tendency to oppress and persecute Christians. The majority of the country's population is Persian and possesses an ancient pre-Islamic culture; it embraced a secularism after the Second World War that inspired many in the greater Islamic world. The Shah ruled the country as a despot from 1941 until 1979, however, and had many internal and external enemies and critics. But in spite of this, Mohammad Rezâ Šâh Pahlavi did promote gender equality, religious tolerance, and an outreach to the West that was a surprising and welcome departure in the region. This overall policy included a tolerance for Iran's Christian minority. He was replaced by the fundamentalism of Ayatollah Khomeini, and the government of the clerics established a brutal and oppressive theocracy, the intensity of which surprised even Sunni hardliners in the Arab world. It was inevitable that the Christian minority of around 250,000 with their 600 churches would be directly affected.

Around half of Iran's Christians live in the capital, Teheran, and most of the rest in the country's other larger cities. There are Assyrian and Armenian Christians in Iran with their own culture and language but also Chaldeans, Presbyterians,

Pentecostals, and other smaller denominations. The experience of Iran's Christians is complex and nuanced. While there is widespread discrimination and persecution, the government – powerful, extensive, and with numerous security agents and police officers – guarantees certain protections. Some Iraqi Christians fleeing Islamist massacres and sectarian brutality following the fall of Saddam Hussein actually found refuge in Iran. But this is no safe haven, and Christians tend to feel increased persecution when international Islam feels slighted or offended. Mobs take to the street, the religious police become more aggressive, and Christians suffer.

One of the most high-profile cases concerned Youcef Nadarkhani, an Iranian Christian pastor who was sentenced to death for the crime of "practising Christianity in Iran" in 2006. It is difficult to know if he was arrested for being a Christian minister or for apostasy – leaving Islam for another religion and for Christianity in particular – which is treated with absolute disdain in Iran. The government media spread the story that his religion was irrelevant and that he was in fact a violent criminal who had raped and stolen but there is no evidence that there is any truth in this whatsoever – such libel is common from the Iranian government. He was arrested again in 2009 after he refused to allow his children to be educated as Muslims in a state school, which was part of a new government educational policy. His wife was arrested shortly afterwards. The case meandered and was layered in distortion, with the Iranians somehow accusing "Zionist media" of making them appear intolerant. Frankly, they didn't need any help. Nadarkhani was a thorn in their side, a Christian who appealed to many young Muslims, and the Iranians were determined to silence him by any means and any charges necessary. They didn't reckon with an international response, which is extremely rare in such cases. Foreign leaders spoke out, international churches campaigned, and North American media for once took an interest in the plight of persecuted Christians.[1]

On September 28, 2011, the Commission on International Religious Freedom, an independent, bipartisan U.S. federal government organization, wrote that "despite the finding that Mr. Nadarkhani did not convert to Christianity as an adult, the [Iranian] court continues to demand that he recant his faith or otherwise be executed. The most recent court proceedings are not only a sham, but are contrary to Iranian law and international human rights standards, including the International Covenant on Civil and Political Rights, to which Iran is a party." Even President Barack Obama, hardly the firmest friend of Christians in Muslim lands, expressed concern on September 30, 2011, saying, "The United States condemns the conviction of Pastor Youcef Nadarkhani. Pastor Nadarkhani has done nothing more than maintain his devout faith, which is a universal right for all people. That the Iranian authorities would try to force him to renounce that faith violates the religious values they claim to defend, crosses all bounds of decency, and breaches Iran's own international obligations." British foreign secretary William Hague added, "I deplore reports that Pastor Youcef Nadarkhani, an Iranian Church leader, could be executed imminently after refusing an order by the Supreme Court of Iran to recant his faith. This demonstrates the Iranian regime's continued unwillingness to abide by its constitutional and international obligations to respect religious freedom. I pay tribute to the courage shown by Pastor Nadarkhani who has no case to answer and call on the Iranian authorities to overturn his sentence." The result was that in 2012, Nadarkhani was formally acquitted of apostasy, convicted of the lesser charge of evangelizing Muslims, but was released for time served. On Christmas Day 2012, he was arrested once again, only to be released two weeks later.

The case demonstrated what can be achieved if people do speak out against persecution, even though Nadarkhani never requested it and even opposed it, preferring to put his fate in God's hands and perhaps by his suffering expose the greater crimes of the Iranian government. He was acutely apolitical and forgiving, refusing even to criticize his tormentors. He wrote at least three letters from prison, a typical passage being this: "What we are bearing today, is a difficult but not unbearable situation, because neither he has tested us more than our faith and our endurance, nor does he do as such. And as we have known from before, we must beware not to fail, but to advance in the grace and knowledge of our Lord and Savior Jesus Christ, And consider these bumps and prisons as opportunities to testify to his name. He said: If anyone is ashamed of me and my words, the Son of Man will be ashamed of him when he comes in his glory and in the glory of the Father and of the holy angels."

Marina Nemat is an author who now lives in Canada but was arrested and tortured in Iran and managed to escape only when one of her interrogators fell in love with her. She was sixteen years old when the police came to take her in the middle of the night. "My parents suffered terribly because they had heard about the rape of young girls and knew about daily mass executions. Every day they waited for the phone call that would tell them to go to the prison gates to collect my belongings because I had been executed." She had been raised a middle-class girl in a secular home, listening to Western pop music and enjoying a comfortable life. Both of her parents worked, she was financially stable, and while a Christian – her grandmothers had been Russian and she was raised with a mingling of Catholicism and Orthodoxy – she was very much an ordinary Iranian. She taught herself English, read voraciously, and wanted to be a doctor. After the Islamic revolution, however, her dreams began to evaporate, her favourite teacher disappeared, and the freedoms she had taken for granted were gradually dismantled and removed. Her father's job had been that of a dance instructor but when the new theocratic government labelled dance as being Western and satanic, he was forced to close his studio and work as a translator. She began to be more political, to think more about her faith, and to protest some of the excesses of the Muslim government. She soon became known to the police and the Revolutionary Guard and shortly afterwards was arrested.

"Persecution of Christians in Iran? This is a big question," she explains. "But just to put it in a nutshell, in practice, the Iranian regime divides Iranian Christians in to 2 groups: 1. Those born in Christian families whose ancestors were Christian or those from other religious minorities who converted to Christianity. 2. Those who have converted to Christianity from Islam. The members of the first group are allowed to practice Christianity and go to church, as long as they do not advertise their religion to Muslims and abide by the laws of the Islamic Republic. However, the members of the second group are considered apostates and would be arrested if discovered. They could even be put to death according to Iranian law. This is why home churches, which have been growing in Iran and which belong to new Christians, have to go underground.

"There are a few contradicting passages when it comes to religious minorities in the Koran. In some of them, Muslims are told to force religious minority into submission and in others it is stated that 'the People of the Book' (Christians, Jews, and Zoroastrians) should be allowed to practice their faith. I must have the Koranic verses somewhere, but you can easily Google them. Basically, the treatment of religious minorities in Muslim countries is a very political issue and depends on that country's interpretation of the Koran and Hadith. I know many practicing Muslims who completely respect religious minorities. Remember, I was not arrested for my faith but I was put in prison because of my outspokenness against the IRI (Islamic Republic of Iran). But when I was in prison and they noticed that I was Christian, the pressure began to mount for me to convert to Islam, to the point that I was threatened. During my time, there were only a handful of Christians in Evin [prison] and we were all there for political reasons."[2]

So in Iran the persecution is different from that in Egypt, Pakistan, Syria, Iraq, and elsewhere. But it is nevertheless real and frightening and always just below the surface. Liana Aghajanian reported in the *New York Times* about a twenty-eight-year-old refugee living in Berlin, Germany. "He converted to Christianity five years ago and spoke to me on condition that I use only his first name [Mori] in order to protect his identity. In 2011, delayed on the way to a secret Bible study session, he narrowly escaped when Revolutionary Guards raided his underground Evangelical church. He watched as his friends disappeared into Iran's prison system; Mori suspects they've been killed.

"'When you're Christian in Iran, you can't speak. You have to keep quiet and not talk about the truth that you know and that you believe in,' he told me. 'There is no such thing as a comfortable life in Iran.' . . .

"Mori was one of the lucky ones. In 2011, he got a fake passport, paid 7,000 euros to a smuggler and joined the rising flow of refugees. The numbers entering Germany, known for its strong record for granting asylum, have soared in recent years, from 815 in 2008 to 4,348 in 2012, and will likely well exceed that figure this year, according to the Association of Iranian Refugees in Berlin. It is difficult to say how many of these people are Christian. A spokeswoman for the federal refugee office told me the government does not keep records on the religious affiliation of applicants. Moreover, Iranians living in cramped conditions in converted schools and barracks are careful to keep their distance from one [another], wary of talking about their cases or their lives back home. Many fear that Iranian government spies have been planted among them, a regular practice of Iran's secret police."[3]

Hamid Pourmand is another high-profile example of Iran's oppression of Christians. He is a convert to the Pentecostal church, having become a Christian in 1980, who is married to an Assyrian Christian; the couple has two boys. As well as being a pastor, Hamid served as an officer in the Iranian army, was a respected soldier, and was quite open about his Christian and evangelical faith and never tried to hide it or subvert the religion of those around him. The problem is that under Iran's Islamic law it is illegal for a non-Muslim to be a military officer. So on September 9, 2004, along with up to eighty-five other church leaders who were attending the annual general conference of the Jama'at-e Rabbani, the largest Pentecostal denomination in Iran, Pourmand was arrested. Every one of the eighty-five Christian delegates was questioned for some time, and it was obvious that the police had extensive information about them and had been following them for some time, including bugging their homes and phones. Many of them, including Pourmand, had had their homes raided and vandalized while they were at the conference and after that had been detained. Most of those arrested were subsequently released but ten pastors, including Pourmand, were held in custody. Those released were warned, threatened, and told not on any account to attend any future or further church meetings. Three days later, the nine other leaders were released but Pourmand was held in prison and prevented from speaking to anybody outside.[4]

He was convicted in February 2006 at a military trial in Teheran of deceiving the army and also of "acts against national security." It was alleged that when he was made an officer, he did not tell the authorities that he had become a Christian, although this was blatantly untrue. He lost his income and pension, his family was thrown into financial trauma, and they assumed they would never see their husband and father again. He was eventually released in 2005, after constant attempts to convert him back to Islam and threats that his return to the Muslim faith was the only way he would escape the death penalty. As the judge was releasing him he said, "I don't know who you are, but apparently the rest of the world does. You must be an important person, because many people from government have called me, saying to cancel your case."

Saeed Abedini is not so lucky. An Iranian-American Christian minister, he has been in the infamous Evin Prison since September 2012 after being sentenced to eight years in prison for undermining national security. Actually Abedini is not political but he is certainly religious, and it was his religious success and establishment of more than a hundred house churches in dozens of Iranian cities that prompted the Iranian government to act. The usual defence from Teheran is that they do not persecute Christians but do disallow dangerous political dissent, and that Abedini and many of his fellow evangelicals are political rather than religious. It's not true. Yet in November, he was moved to the violent and infamous Rajai Shahr prison, living with prisoners serving life sentences for murder. It is unsure whether he will survive.

Mehdi Dibaj did not. He was a Christian convert from Sunni Islam, itself a minority religion in Iran. He became a Pentecostal Christian as a young man, long before the Iranian Revolution. After sharia law was applied, however, he was placed under police surveillance and regularly harassed. He was abducted on Friday, June 24, 1994, and his body was found on July 5. The *Independent* newspaper in Britain remembered him in an obituary.

Dibaj became a Christian as a young man and joined the Assemblies of God Church, later becoming an evangelist. Following the 1979 Iranian Revolution he encountered problems. In 1983 he was arrested and imprisoned without trial in the town of Sari in north-eastern Iran. He was systematically tortured. For two years of his imprisonment he was held in solitary confinement in an unlit cell measuring 3ft by 3ft. He was finally tried by an Islamic court in Sari on 3 December last year and later in the month was sentenced to death on charges of "apostasy" – in Islamic law a crime carrying the death penalty. . . .

Following a world-wide outcry Dibaj was finally freed in January, although the sentence of death was not lifted. Just three days later his friend Bishop Haik Hovsepian Mehr

– who had campaigned for Dibaj's freedom – was abducted and murdered.

During Hovsepian Mehr's funeral on 3 February, Dibaj declared: "I should have died, not Brother Haik."

Dibaj disappeared on 24 June. According to the Iranian police, his body was found in a park in west Tehran on Tuesday while they were searching for the killers of another pastor, Tateos Michaelian.[5]

The man of whom he spoke, Haik Hovsepian Mehr, was a bishop who in the 1980s and early '90s publicly defended Iranian Christians and became a beacon for passive resistance to the government's oppression of Christianity. He found himself in particular trouble when he refused to comply with increasingly strident government restrictions on Christian activity and then objected to a new code that Teheran had insisted upon. It demanded that "Church services could not be held in Persian, the official language of Iran; Church members must be issued membership cards and produce them upon attendance; Membership lists, complete with addresses, must be handed over to governmental authorities; Meetings must be confined to Sunday, not Friday the officially recognized day of Muslim worship; Only members could attend Sunday meetings; and new members could only be added to the membership and admitted to meetings once the Ministry of Information and Islamic Guidance had been notified."

He also launched a campaign for the release of his friend and co-religionist Mehdi Dibaj, whom we described above. The campaign was partly successful, and when Dibaj was released, those who had arrested and incarcerated him were outraged and clearly set on vengeance. Just three days after the release,

Hovsepian disappeared. His family and friends searched for him but were given very little help from the authorities. His body was found at the end of January 1994. The government still blithely denies any responsibility.

It is impossible for the Iranians to deny that they were responsible for the death of Hossein Soodmand because he was executed by the state in 1989 for the crime of apostasy. He left behind a wife who was blind and four children. Many Iranian Christian leaders and foreign diplomats had called for clemency but the government's ombudsman insisted that he be hanged. His family was not allowed to care for or bury his body. One of his children, Rashin Soodmand, still campaigns for her father's memory and legacy. She told journalist Mark Ellis that when her father was just seven years old, he broke the water bucket of a Christian woman with a stone by accident.

As soon as he saw it break, he turned to run, but tripped over a large stone, crashed on the ground, and blood began to ooze out of his knee.

Then he saw the Christian woman move towards him and fear gripped his heart. There was no escape. He had thrown the stones. He deserved the punishment. Now her shadow loomed over him and he expected her to strike in anger.

But something astonishing happened. Instead of angry blows, her hand reached down and helped him to his feet and the "unclean" Christian woman cleaned his wound. . . .

Years later, during Hossein's two-year military service, he got very sick and had to go to the hospital. An Armenian Christian friend came to see him and left him a cross as a parting gift. That night Hossein had a vivid dream about

Jesus Christ. Jesus gave the young man something to eat. The next morning, Hossein woke up sweating and realized Jesus had touched him and brought healing to his body. . . .

But the storm clouds of persecution that followed the Islamic revolution gathered over the budding fellowship. The church was often forced to close and Rev. Soodmand and other believers were arrested multiple times by the religious police. They suffered psychological and physical torture. . . .

When the religious police saw they could not silence Hossein, the persecution increased. One day they came to his house and offered an ultimatum: "Either deny your faith and stop what you are doing or we will kill you," they said. "You have two weeks to think about it."

Hossein met with church leaders in Tehran who offered to help him and his family escape Iran. His response was full of the sacrificial love demonstrated by his Savior.[6]

Saba Farzan from the Institute for Middle Eastern Democracy has written that "the situation of Christians and other religious minorities in Iran is very dire because the Iranian regime is a Sharia state. This dictatorship oppresses viciously all these precious groups with the abhorrent justification of Islamic law and by that it violates Iran's constitution and a long-lasting tradition within Persian culture of peaceful tolerance and respect towards fellow Iranians with diverse religious backgrounds."

So this isn't the daily grind of mob violence, gang rapes, beatings, and discrimination that the Christians of Pakistan, Syria, or Egypt experience but a government policy that will tolerate Christians only if they are born into the faith and keep it firmly within the walls of their state-approved church. It's a well-considered policy in that the government knows that new, young blood is coming from converts and an evangelicalism that defines itself largely by outreach and public witness. The ayatollahs want to see established Christians leave or die natural deaths and for their churches to gradually disappear; by firmly suppressing new, more youthful churches, they believe they can hasten the death of the Christian faith in Iran. The courage of all Iranian Christians is awe-inspiring but that of the country's Pentecostal Christians in particular is remarkable, their treatment remarkably cruel.

INDONESIA

ONE WOULD HAVE THOUGHT, OR hoped, that the situation in Indonesia was different from that in the Middle East or South Asia. The cultural traditions of the region are more pluralistic, the political system more democratic, and the social context less controlled. Around 10 per cent of the population is Christian – 7 per cent Protestant and 3 per cent Catholic; 86 per cent of Indonesia is Muslim. Because of Indonesia's geographical composition and it being an archipelago composed of more than 13,000 islands, the Christian population is spread and not evenly distributed. Sumatra is mostly Muslim, Java varies between 5 and 12 per cent Christian, and in the West, Central, and East Kalimantan provinces the Christian population is as high as a third. The Chinese population is the most Christian, with the official numbers being around 35 per cent but probably far more actually being Christian. Indonesia has the largest Muslim population in the world.

The country was founded on the philosophy of Pancasila, composed of two ancient Javanese words meaning "five" and "principles." The five include a belief in God but the God in question is not specified; a just and civilized society; unity; democracy; and social justice. An admirable and splendid policy that stood firm for half a century and is still proclaimed and supported by many in government and within the Indonesian population and establishment. But, tragically, in the last years of the twentieth and first years of the twenty-first centuries the situation has changed radically. An anti-Christian war by Islamists intent on bringing all of Indonesia under sharia law is going strong, and it's estimated that more than 30,000 Christians have been killed and perhaps half a million forced from their homes. The government is having some success with its anti-terror and anti-Islamist campaign but the situation is still unstable and dangerous. During the worst of the jihadist terror there were forced circumcisions, rapes, beheadings, and tor-ture, and the army and police were often accused of abetting Islamists. Churches and Christian graveyards have been van-dalized, holy sites destroyed, Christians denied jobs and uni-versity places, and entire communities forcibly removed by terror and violence.[1]

Because of the geography of Indonesia and the relative iso-lation of some of its Christians, the violence is extreme and shocking even by Islamist standards. In October 2001 in Peleru, Islamists murdered ten Christians and injured dozens more, and in the same month in Tomata three women were killed when their church was attacked. Also in October a Christian was dragged from his car and slaughtered on the side of the road. In December in Kapaha nine Christians on a boat were murdered, and then in Ewiri three Christians were killed. In Sepe in December six Christians were chased from their own homes and killed, and the rest of the year saw attacks in Ambon, Palu, Tomata, and Waimulang. More than fifteen Christians were killed in these attacks, and in two of them the roads were blocked by men in uniform who then singled out Christians and promptly killed them. In 2002 in January in Malei a Christian was shot dead by a Muslim gang while he was picking fruit, and then in Palu a coordinated bomb attack in four separate churches injured several worshippers and killed one man. In April a particularly violent attack occurred. According to the BBC, "At least 12 people have been killed by a Muslim mob which attacked a Christian village in the Moluccan islands in eastern Indonesia. The violence then spread to the regional capital, Ambon city, where a bomb went off, and a centre for Christian and Muslim children and one of the city's main churches were set on fire. The violence began early on Sunday in the village of Soya. 'They attacked the village by using home-made bombs and set fire to some of the houses,' a local journalist said. There are reports that some 30 homes and a church were set on fire. Six people are reported to have been stabbed to death, and a further six are said to have died in the fires. Christian sources say the Soya attack was carried out by a Muslim mob armed with machetes, knives and bombs. Many of the villagers, particularly the women and children, have now fled the area."

Later in April in Ambon a bomb was thrown into a Christian centre with more than fifty people being injured and five killed. Two months later in Tentena a church bus was bombed and four people were killed, including the church's minister, and more than a dozen people were badly hurt. The year 2002 was an appalling one for Indonesia's Christians. In Saparua five were killed and eleven wounded in an attack on a boat, in Wayura a Christian fisherman was murdered, in Landangan a man walking home was shot dead, and in Matako a pogrom took place when a large number of Muslim men and youths stormed the village and burned churches and homes while shooting at anyone they assumed to be a Christian. They were chanting Muslim slogans as they did so. In Mayoa three Christians were killed, in Kawua another bus was attacked with one person killed, in Malei two people were killed in an attack on two neighbouring villages, and in Manyomba a group of more than fifty Muslims attacked Christian villages and murdered three people. They also strangled a three-year-old to death. In Kayamanya five Christians were killed in a bus and car attack, in Kelang two people were killed and another two wounded in a gun attack, and in Galunggung a Christian man was beaten by a Muslim mob and then burned to death.[2]

At the beginning of 2003 in Wamena a significant assault took place because it involved not mobs and gangs but the uniformed military, who raided Christian villages, desecrated Bibles, and killed at least fifteen people, two of them Baptist ministers. They also beat and tortured any other Christians they could find. Soldiers and policemen had undoubtedly been involved in earlier attacks but had never identified themselves as such. Not this time. It was bold and brutal and a clear statement was being made.

In Kapompa a Christian was killed and another injured, in Marowo in May a Muslim man was killed because he was with his Christian brother-in-law, and in Kawua a restaurant owned by a Christian family was bombed and five people hurt. In July in Sulawesi a Christian farmer was shot dead while working in his field, and in October in Pandiri a forty-four-year-old man was murdered because he had converted from Islam to Christianity. In the same month in Sulawesi a mass attack took place and eight Christians were murdered, a church was burned and many other worshippers badly injured. The last months of the year were equally brutal. In Poso in October Christian homes were burned and two men killed, in Sulawesi in three attacks in October and November a Christian farmer was killed, a Christian was dragged from his motorcycle and beaten to death, and then a church worker was shot dead and his young nephew who was with him was also murdered. At the beginning of 2004 in Palopo four Christians were killed and several others injured when a café frequented by local Christians was bombed. It was not the first, nor would it be the last, time that this particular café was targeted. There were two more attacks in Maranatha in the early months of 2004. In the first the leader of the local Christian community, a middle-aged man, was killed by local Muslims who had known him for many years; in the second a mother of two was killed with a machete by a Muslim angry at what he said was her denial of Mohammad. In Tomura in March a Christian minister was shot dead in his church as his wife tried to save him, and also in March in Poso a young Christian man was shot dead on the street as he walked home. In April in Sulawesi during an Easter service a gang of Muslims opened fire on a church and injured seven people – it was extraordinary that nobody was killed. In Posu another Easter service was attacked in a similar style, again with injuries but no deaths. The following month in Maluku Islamists stole a speedboat and used it as a gun plat-form from which they shot at Christians and killed a man and a baby of less than a year; three other people were wounded.

In Ambon in late April there was a mass attack. According to Matthew Moore, Indonesia correspondent of Melbourne's *The Age*: "Survivors of an attack by an armed gang that left about 20 people injured in Indonesia's Maluku province have accused the Indonesian security forces of standing by while men, women and children were stoned and attacked with machetes and clubs. . . . But when the group of Ambon residents climbed onto two trucks provided by Indonesia's para-military police Brimob, a gang of men surrounded them and began stoning them while the security forces in a third truck looked on. 'They (security forces) were only 10 metres away.

They did nothing to help us, we were extremely disappointed. It was as if that was their intention,' he told *The Age* at Bakti Rahayu hospital. Mr Makatita suffered only a head wound, but his sister Seli, who is six months pregnant, was stabbed in the back and slashed with a machete on the lower and upper arm as well as the chin. In a makeshift hospital set up in a church, Seli's mother told how she was slashed with a machete on her neck when young men tried to cut her throat while she was protecting her three-year-old granddaughter. 'The police did not do anything. People were screaming for help and crying as they were attacked.'"[3]

In Palu in March a Christian lawyer was murdered because he was working within the state legal system to oppose the appeal of three jihadists who had been given prison sentences for carrying out bomb outrages against innocent Christians. Also in Palu in July gunmen ran into a church and killed a woman pastor and a teenage girl; three others people were shot but didn't die. In October in Jono Oge in a brazen attack in the middle of a crowded street a Muslim mob armed with swords and knives killed two Christians, and in the same month in Sulawesi two Christian men were shot and their Hindu friend killed. In Poso in two attacks a guard at a Catholic church was killed and then mujahideen terrorists decapitated the leader of the local Christian community. At the end of 2004 and beginning of 2005 there was a series of attacks in Sulawesi. First, three worshippers were killed in a church attack, then six Christians were murdered by their Muslim neighbours because they refused to convert to Islam. In a horrendous attack in Tentena around twenty-five people were killed, including a priest and a child, when Islamists bombed buildings and areas where they knew Christians gathered. A local police official said at the time that "Tentena is considered as a safe haven for Christians, and many from out of town had found sanctuary there in the past to avoid the violent communal conflicts with the Muslim population." There was clearly nowhere left to be safe.[4]

In Maluku in May five police officers who were accused of protecting a Christian village were murdered in their sleep by Muslims. In August in Poso two people who had appeared as witnesses in a court case against Islamists who had launched a terror attack against Christians were murdered; this was the latest in a pattern of attacks on lawyers and witnesses working to convict terrorists. In the same month in Ambon seven Christians were hurt when a bomb exploded in the Christian quarter of the town, in October in Pantangolemba a middle-aged Christian man was shot dead, and in Landangan a forty-three-year-old Christian was murdered. Then in October in Bukit Bambu an event occurred that caused international horror. Dan McDougall in the *Guardian* wrote poignantly of the situation:

"First light is the most captivating time of day as you cross the vastness of the Indonesian archipelago. Set against the blood-orange horizon, the echoing call of the muezzin shakes you from your dreamlike state as men file to morning prayers in bleary-eyed procession. Islanders arch their backs against heavy carts laden with fresh jackfruit and laughing children in white uniforms dawdle to school. But in the central towns of the Indonesian island of Sulawesi events of the past few weeks have destroyed the frivolity of the pupils' daily journeys. Three weeks ago, four cousins from the tightly-knit Christian community, Theresia Morangke, 15, Alfita Poliwo, 17, Yarni Sambue, 17, and Noviana Malewa, 15, were brutally attacked as they walked to the Central Sulawesi Christian Church High

School by men wearing black ski masks. Three of the girls were beheaded. Noviana, the youngest, survived, despite appalling machete wounds to her neck. The headless bodies of her cousins were dumped beside a busy nearby road. Two of the heads were found several kilometres away in the suburb of Lege. The third, Theresia's, was left outside a recently built Christian church in the village of Kasiguncu. A week after the attack, a day after Alfita's funeral, two other Christian girls, Ivon Maganti and Siti Nuraini, both 17, were shot by masked men as they walked to a Girl Scouts' meeting. They and Noviana are still critically ill in hospital. All six were Christians in a predominantly Muslim community. And yesterday police in Sulawesi said two young women had been attacked on Friday by black-clad assailants on motorbikes armed with machetes."

He went on to quote a lay preacher in the town called David, who lamented, "Pope Benedict led prayers in Rome for the safety of Christians here, but few governments have expressed real concern. We are on the verge of another jihad. Almost all the religiously motivated aggression this year has been directed against Christians: schoolgirls murdered as the army turns a blind eye. But the government would rather talk of gangsters, not jihadists, carrying out the attacks. I want to know why most of the weapons carried by these militants are army issue." MacDougall added that, "To Christians such as David it is 'unthinkable' that the military could have failed to end the attacks. Similar failures can be discerned in other Indonesian hotspots, including Maluku, and the West Kalimantan town of Sambas, where Christians have also been targeted. Claims of army complicity are rife among Christians, who regularly accuse the military of turning a blind eye to the Islamic militia in the area and the smuggling of weapons from the mainland.

Others point to a lack of prosecutions for attacks on Christians and talk darkly of militant training camps in remote valleys, as if to say the next mass slaughter is just around the corner. 'There is a pattern,' says Mona Saroinsong, co-ordinator of the Protestant Church Crisis Centre in Manado, North Sulawesi. 'There have been other attacks apart from the beheadings and shootings and none of the aggressors has been found. The attackers operate in small groups, each with a specific task and area to cover, and wear black masks to avoid being identified. Another similarity with previous attacks is that the head of the police was elsewhere when the killers struck.'"

When the killers were caught, their testimony was chilling. They said they had beheaded the girls as a Ramadan "trophy" and had also left a note that read: "Wanted: 100 more Christian heads, teenaged or adult, male or female; blood shall be answered with blood, soul with soul, head with head." They also boasted that the beheading was "an act of Muslim charity."[5]

One might have thought that the intensity and darkness of the beheadings might have slowed down the Islamist attacks but the contrary was the case. In November in Palu an innocent Christian couple were murdered on their way to church, and in the same month in Poso two Christian seventeen-year-old-year-old girls were shot dead. In Sulawesi in December eight Christians were killed when a nail-bomb was detonated in a market. The particular part of the market was targeted because it contained stalls selling pork and the Islamists knew there would only be Christians present.

In 2006 in Ambon a Catholic nun was stabbed to death, in Tangkuran a Christian man was murdered, and in Poso in October a man was pulled from a bus by a Muslim mob and beaten and stabbed to death because he was identified as a

Christian. Also in October, in Sulawesi, a Christian pastor was killed while his wife was forced to watch. In June 2007 in Pekanbaru a Christian teacher was killed in front of his little son, and, in Horale in February 2008 three people were killed and numerous homes and churches burned when a Muslim mob stormed through the village. In Jakarta in June Christians were attacked with machetes and in July in the same city more than 200 people were injured when a large mob attacked a Christian school. This in turn led to further violence. Asia News reported shortly afterwards that, "Last night hundreds of residents from the village of Kampung Pulo had taken up arms threatening to storm the school after being instigated by an imam at a local mosque who claimed that a bunch of Christian gangsters were coming to 'protect' the school after it was attacked on Saturday by a Muslim mob, causing damage to the building and hurting hundreds."[6] It seems that Indonesian Christians are damned if they are attacked, damned if they try to defend themselves.

In Bekasi in August Christians were chased and attacked after they left a church service, and the following month in the same town a minister and a worshipper were attacked as they walked to church, the latter being stabbed in the stomach. In Temanggung a priest was beaten up after he tried to stop a mob burning his church, and then in East Java a Christian woman was kidnapped, cut with a knife, and held prisoner for two days. In Malei in August 2011 a man was killed after his home had been vandalized by Muslims, and in the same month in Sepe five people were killed and homes and churches destroyed when a Christian district was attacked. In September in Maluku six Christians were killed with machetes, and then in Solo a young girl and two older people were killed when a nail-bomb was detonated in their church. In October 2012 in

Masani two detectives investigating a church bombing were themselves killed by Islamists when they were stabbed in the neck and their throats cut.

In the past two years the government has been more efficient in countering Islamist terror and has certainly been more determined in taking a firm stand. Some of the leaders of the jihadists have also moved to other areas, fighting in Syria, Chechnya, and any other areas where Muslim groups are engaged in military campaigns. While organized and well-armed attacks have declined, random street attacks have continued. It's also sadly the case that isolated Christian communities have abandoned their towns and villages for the safety of large towns with more stable and sizeable Christian centres. To that extent the Islamists have been successful. In Christian-majority areas, Christians are usually safe; in Muslim-majority areas their security is never guaranteed. Beyond the violence there is discrimination in employment, in trying to obtain permits to build churches, and in promotion in the bureaucracy and government service. The government might be opposed to the jihadists but it is hardly secular. In 2013, for example, two Christian brothers, Kashfi and Jalaudin Rosyid, were arrested after a mob of more than two hundred Muslims attacked their home, angry at an evangelization campaign that had converted dozens of Muslims to Christianity. The police managed to rescue the two men but they were then charged with proselytizing. They were tried, convicted, and sentenced to three years in prison. It's reported that in prison they are beaten and bullied and seldom protected by the warders and governor.

So contemporary Indonesia is not the country founded on those five glorious principles of the 1940s, especially for its long-suffering Christian minority.

AFRICA

CHRISTIANITY IS, OF COURSE, widespread and dynamic in Africa, as is Islam and – unfortunately – violence against Christians. The situation varies from country to country and region to region, but I have chosen to discuss Nigeria for two specific reasons. First, it is the country in sub-Saharan Africa where anti-Christian terror is at its worst; second, Nigeria has a dramatically different power and population ratio from the other nations we have considered. Unlike Pakistan, Indonesia, Egypt, Syria, Iraq, and Iran, Nigeria is around half Christian, and the Christian population may even be as high as 54 per cent. The southern and central regions of the country are dominated by Christians, and as many as 85 million Nigerians are Christian, making it by population numbers the most Christian country in Africa; in percentage terms, however, the most Christian country on the continent would be Angola. There are around 19 million Catholics in Nigeria, 17 million Anglicans, and 4 million Presbyterians. There is also the National Church of Nigeria, the Evangelical Reformed Church, the Mormons, around 6 million Baptists, and numbers of Jehovah's Witnesses, Pentecostals, and other denominations. Since the late 1990s, there have been widespread Islamist attacks on all of these groups in the north of the country, with more than 1,500 people killed in the first three months of 2014 alone and almost 4,000 murdered between 2010 and the end of 2013.[1]

The terror campaign is known as the Islamist Insurgency in Nigeria or the Sharia Conflict and has its origins in the fact that while Nigeria's constitution is secular and there is supposed to be a separation of church and state or mosque and state, twelve individual states were allowed to apply sharia law between 1999 and 2012. Nine state have full sharia law – Zamfara, Kano, Sokoto, Katsina, Bauchi, Borno, Jigawa, Kebbi, and Yobe – and three – Kaduna, Niger, and Gombe – have sharia applied in parts of the state. This led to confrontations between Christians and Muslims, which in turn led to an organized and extremely violent campaign spearheaded by the Islamist group Boko Haram, or "Western education is sinful," although the official name of the group is the Congregation of the People of Tradition for Proselytism and Jihad. Boko Haram is responsible for much, but certainly not all, of the violence that has taken place against Christians, and that violence has been occurring for more than fifteen years.

From the end of 2001, the situation has deteriorated enormously. In December in Vwang, five Christians were killed and the town was largely destroyed. The following year, 2012, began with an attack in Ilorin in which three Christians were killed. In Gombi, a young woman was kidnapped and had her throat cut; she was left to bleed to death and suffered for some time before she died. In March in Enugu, twelve Christians were murdered when a prayer service was attacked, and in June in Katsina, a Christian policeman was beaten to death after being accused of desecrating the Koran, which he almost certainly did not do. In October in Zaria, twenty Christian students were killed by a Muslim mob, and in the same month in Fajul, a mass attack took place with the slaughter of more than forty Christians, the rape of women, and the burning of churches. In Rim in December, thirteen people were killed, and in Kaduna, a massacre occurred that was almost surreal in its origins. The BBC reported, "The troubles began with a protest by Muslims in Kaduna last Wednesday over a newspaper article they saw as trivializing their objections to the [Miss World beauty] contest, and escalated on Thursday when the worst of the violence appears to have taken place. . . . Nigeria won the right to stage the pageant after Nigerian Agbani Darego was crowned Miss World 2001 – the first black African to win the title."[2] Muslims objected to the competition taking place in Nigeria and were then provoked to rioting and violence when a newspaper article suggested that Mohammad might well have married one of the contestants if he was alive today. While Muslims also died in the violence, it was Islamic militants who started the confrontation, burned down churches, and committed most of the violence and killing.[3]

In March 2003 in Kadarko, twenty-two Christians were killed and dozens more injured, and in April in Fobur, several houses were burned down and a woman killed. A few days later in Kano, a Christian minister, his wife, and three children were killed, and in Numan, a woman pastor was stabbed to death. In Yelwa in February 2004, forty-nine Christians were killed, mainly hacked to death, when they fled a Muslim mob and hid in a church. In April in Rwang Doka and Jenkur, there were coordinated attacks and three people were killed. May was a terrible month. In Kano, thirty people were killed in a single day and another eleven the following day when two churches were burned. In Saminka, seven Christians were killed; in Jiram, another fifteen were murdered; in Sabo Gida, another ten; in Bakin Ciyawa, twenty-four people were slaughtered; in Gidan Sabo, eighteen were killed, and another three in

Langtang. The year ended with an attack in Jigawa that led to two deaths, and in Bauchi a Christian student was kidnapped from his college and murdered. In Demsa in 2005, more than thirty Christians were killed and thousands exiled – ethnic cleansing being a key factor in the Islamist campaigns. There were other attacks in Numan, Benue, and Niger Province. The number of attacks and numbers killed in them is breathtaking.

Potiskum and Kontagora were raided in early 2006 resulting in numerous deaths and damage, and in Bauchi in February, more than twenty-five people were killed when organized mobs attacked Christian villages. The devastation continued in February. Maiduguri saw the deaths of thirty Christians, then Borno was attacked after the Danish cartoon of Mohammad was published – similar attacks occurred in Maiduguri, where sixteen people were murdered and numerous churches were burned. In the summer, Kumutu was targeted and three people were killed. In 2007 in Kano, ten Christians were murdered; one of the victims was a Catholic priest. In Bauchi in October, three churches were burned down and ten Christians killed; in Gamji Gate, two Christians were killed, one with a sword. Jos was attacked in 2008, with eight people dying in two major attacks, and in 2009 Bauchi and then Maiduguri were hit, the latter in three separate attacks. Nigeria's Christians assumed that matters could not get worse. They were wrong.

According to Adam Nossiter of the *New York Times*:

Officials and human rights groups in Nigeria sharply increased the count of the dead after a weekend of vicious ethnic violence, saying Monday that as many as 500 people – many of them women and children – may have been killed near the city of Jos, long a center of tensions between Christians and Muslims. . . .

A few miles south of the city nearly 400 of the victims were buried in a mass grave in Dogon Na Hauwa, the village where the worst violence occurred. Some of the bodies had been mutilated.

There, women cried inconsolably amid crowds of mourners, and the smell of burned and decomposing flesh hung in the air. Officials combed a large area around the village, continuing to find bodies during the day.[4]

In Dyie, thirteen Christians were killed and had their tongues cut out, and in Jos, three Christians were murdered during a march for peace. The rest of the year saw killings, arson, and beatings in Riyom, Boto, Ganawuri, Kizachi, Chewenkur, and Turu. On Christmas Eve in Jos – a place of unimaginable pain and fear now – more than eighty people died in a number of bomb attacks timed to detonate during Christmas Eve services. People fleeing the explosions were hacked to death.[5]

There were dozens of attacks in 2011 all over northern Nigeria, the worst being in Kaduna and Potiskum, where hundreds were killed. The year 2012 was similar, with dozens of Islamist attacks. It is genuinely difficult to single out particular attacks and incidents as the violence and indifference to human life is so constant and repetitive. In Potiskum, for example, six Christians were killed by machine-gun fire while they were sitting on a bus at a gas station. The dead included a woman and a baby. In Maiduguri, two attacks occurred in the space of just a few weeks, with two Christians dying in each incident. In Adamawa, twelve people were killed while at prayer in a church, and another twenty were killed in Mubi at a funeral. In Gombe, another church was attacked and nine people were killed, including the minister's wife and family. In Tafawa Balewa, grenades were thrown into the homes of Christians and several were killed; some of those fleeing in panic were shot dead. There were attacks in Sulieja, Potiskum, and Maiduguri, with several fatalities; in the latter, the seventy-five-year-old mother of a local minister had her throat cut. In Jos, a suicide bomber killed four people at a church service, one of the dead a baby. In Nayi, ten Christians were shot and hacked to death; in Bilala, a church was bombed and two people killed; and in Benue, twenty-one Christians, mostly women and children, were killed with machetes by an Islamic gang. In Maiduguri, there were two attacks, with nine people killed in a market bombing and then another shot as he left his church. In Kaduna at Easter, a suicide bomber killed more than thirty-five people and injured many more; in Kanu, sixteen people, many of them members of the local Christian middle class, including doctors and academics, were shot as they fled their church after it was bombed. In Adamawa, fifteen Christians were massacred, and in Tahoss seven people, two of them small children, were shot.

In On-Mbaagbu, two villages were attacked and seven people, one a two-year-old, were killed with knives, and in Bauchi a car was driven at high speed into a prayer service and twenty people were killed. In Jos, a suicide bomber killed four people in a church, and in Trikania, another suicide bomber in an explosives-packed car smashed his way into a church and killed five people. In Zaria, nineteen people were killed and dozens wounded when Islamists launched coordinated attacks. According to Reuters:

There was no immediate claim of responsibility for the bombings, but the Islamist group Boko Haram has often attacked church services in Nigeria, which is split roughly evenly between Christians and Muslims. . . .

On the previous Sunday, militants attacked two churches in Nigeria, spraying the congregation of one of them with bullets, killing at least one person, and blowing up a car in a suicide bombing at the other, wounding 41. Boko Haram claimed responsibility.

In the latest violence, the first two blasts hit churches in the town of Zaria within minutes of each other. In the first attack, a suicide bomber drove a blue Honda Civic into Ekwa Church, said its pastor, the Rev. Nathan Waziri. The second suicide car bombing was at Kings Catholic Church, killing 10 people, said Bishop George Dogo of Zaria.

Suicide bombers in a Toyota sedan then hit Shalom Church in the state's main city, Kaduna, killing six people. Manan Janet, who was in the church, said she saw six bodies. "It was terrible," she said. "I'm traumatized."[6]

In July 2012, at least twenty-three people were killed in Plateau state; numbers are sometimes difficult to verify and are often higher than reported. More than two hundred Islamists, armed with guns and machetes, attacked two villages and began their slaughter, and when the police and military tried to intervene and stop the violence, they were attacked as well. In Barkin-Ladi, twenty-three Christians were killed while they attended a funeral for past victims of Muslim terror. In Okene, a group of Islamists broke into a church and opened fire with machine guns. Nineteen people were killed, including the minister. In Riyom, twelve people were killed, three of them children. In Mubi, Islamists raided a campus and carefully seg-regated the Christians from the Muslims, twenty-six of the former being shot and having their throats cut. In Yogbo, thirty Christians were killed; in Madauchi-Zonkwa, a Christian family was burned to death in their home, and in Jali, a pair of suicide bombers killed fifteen people in a Protestant church. The year ended with a plague of violence. In Bichi, four Christians were killed after an argument concerning a T-shirt one of them was wearing that was considered to be blasphem-ous; in Maiduguri, an octogenarian retired minister was mur-dered; in Peri on Christmas morning, five worshippers were killed in their church; in Rim, another Christmas service was raided; in Maiduguri, another six Christians were killed while at Christmas mass; and at Kyachi, fifteen worshippers were held at gunpoint, tied up, and shot one by one.

In February 2013 in Abuja, there was a major attack when Islamists razed a factory and systematically separated the Muslim from the Christian workers. Seventeen of the Christians who had been taken aside were then shot dead. In Kogom, ten members of the same family were hacked to death, and in Fika, five people were killed as a Muslim mob ran through a Christian village shooting and stabbing. In Aduwan, a baby and teenager were among the victims when Islamists entered a church and fired their machine guns, and in Dakata, five Christians were murdered on their way home from church. In Jama'are, another seven Christians were killed; in Torok in March, three women, a five-year-old, and a baby were shot but survived. Also in March in Ataka, nineteen people were killed, in Barkin Ladi another nine, and in Riyom more than thirty Christians were slaughtered in a mass attack. The following month in Gwoza, three Christians were shot dead, and in Midlu Shalmi, fourteen people were murdered. In May in Mjilan, a church and a cattle market frequented by Christians were raided and ten Christians were killed. There were further attacks in the same month in Borno and Gwoza. In June in Bakin Rijiya, four churches were burned and a worshipper killed, and in September in Adu, nine Christians, two of them children, were machine-gunned. In Jos, another five people were murdered, and in Nasarawa, a church was attacked by Islamists with knives and clubs and several people were beaten and stabbed. In Zangang, a well-armed group of Muslim militia raided a village and hacked fifteen people to death. There were further attacks in Dorawa and Rantis, and then in Barkin Ladi in November, thirty-seven Christians in four separate villages were shot and killed; several children and pregnant women were among the dead. In more attacks in Kula, five Christians were killed, in Gwol six were killed, in Arkobo four were killed, in Kwajffa another four were killed, and in Maikatako on New Year's Eve at a special church service three people were shot dead.

The year 2014 started with the same degree of violence and anti-Christian terror. In January in Waga Chakawa, Islamist militias obviously decided to make a statement. Reuters reported:

Suspected insurgents armed with guns and explosives killed at least 62 people in northeast Nigeria, including at a church service, in a region where Islamist sect Boko Haram is resisting a military crackdown, witnesses said on Monday.

They killed 22 people by setting off bombs and firing into the congregation in the Catholic church in Waga Chakawa village in Adamawa state on Sunday, before burning houses and taking residents hostage during a four-hour siege, witnesses said. . . .

The spokesman for the Catholic Diocese of Yola, Reverend Father Raymond Danbouye, confirmed 22 people killed in the church were buried at a funeral on Monday. . . .

Several witnesses put the figure at 50, although none had counted the numbers of bodies themselves. They added that the militants had burned down the village and set off multiple explosions, shooting anyone trying to flee.

"The whole village has been razed by Boko Haram and there were still loud explosions from different directions as I left, with bodies littering the village," said resident Bulama Kuliri, who narrowly escaped.[7]

In Agatu, seven people were killed when their village was set alight; in Sabon Gari, seven people were killed and others badly injured. In Garin Yamdula, a minister and ten members of his church were murdered, and in Unguwar Kajit, seven Christians were killed in their own home by Islamist gunmen. In Izghe, a virtual pogrom took place in February. According to the BBC, "Suspected Islamist militants have raided a Nigerian village and murdered dozens, according to witnesses. The gunmen reportedly rounded up a group of men in Izghe village and shot them, before going door-to-door and killing anyone they found. . . . The senator for Borno state, where the attack took place, told the BBC's Newsday programme that 106 people – 105 men and an elderly woman trying to protect her grandson – were killed in the latest attack. Ali Ndume said around 100 Islamist militants attacked Izghe for five hours on Saturday evening, without any intervention from the army. He said the military recently withdrew from the area after nine soldiers were killed in an ambush last week. Residents who fled the attack in Izghe said some of the victims were shot, while others had their throats slit. 'All the dead bodies of the victims are still lying in the streets,' resident Abubakar Usman told Reuters news agency. 'We fled without burying them, fearing the terrorists were still lurking in the bushes.' Other witnesses described how the attackers had arrived on Saturday evening in trucks and motorcycles. They asked the men in the village to gather, and then they hacked and shot them to death."[8]

In Adamawa, more than thirty people were killed, and in Michika at the end of February, another three were murdered. The Morning Star News reported that in March in Chenshyi, "Muslim herdsmen armed with guns and machetes on Friday night launched attacks on three villages in Kaduna state, killing more than 100 Christians and destroying homes, sources said.

"Scores of the ethnic Fulani assailants simultaneously attacked the Christian villages of Ugwar Sankwai, Ungwar Gata and Chenshyi in the Kaura Local Government Area for about four hours, sources said. The Rev. Yakubu Gandu Nkut, chairman of the Zankan area chapter of the Christian Association of Nigeria (CAN), told Morning Star News that a pastor's wife and her three children were among the dead.

"'The unfortunate attack on our communities has led to killing of more than 100 Christians,' Nkut said. 'The wife of one of our pastors, Mrs. Jummai Likita Riku, and her three children, from the ECWA [Evangelical Church Winning All] church, Ugwar Sankwai, were killed in the attack.'

"ECWA and Anglican church buildings were burned down by the herdsmen in Ugwar Sankwai, Nkut said. . . . In Manchok, where several Christians have taken refuge, Nuhu Moses of Chenshyi village told reporters that the Muslim Fulani herdsmen killed about 50 Christians.

"'The cattlemen who attacked my village were more than 40 – they were armed with guns and other weapons,' Moses told Morning Star News. 'As I talk to you, there is no single house that has not been destroyed as the attackers set fire on our houses. As we made efforts to escape from being killed, our attackers shot at every one they saw. It was a miracle that I escaped alive.'"[9]

There were more attacks in Riyom with sixteen killed; in Taraba, with thirty-five killed in a Catholic church; and in Gbajimba, with another thirty-six people murdered. Then in April, Boko Haram kidnapped nearly two hundred boarding school girls in a coordinated attack. Christian Association of Nigerian-Americans executive director pastor Laolu Akande explained at the time that the strategy is not in fact something new. "Boko Haram has been kidnapping little girls who are Christians, trying to turn them into sex slaves, trying to convert them by force. Their strategy is to marry the girls and kill the men. So what they have done by kidnapping these female students, it is another demonstration of the impunity with which Boko Haram has been running its terrorist activities." He said that in 2012, Boko Haram entered the home of a Christian woman named Deborah Shettima from Borno state, killed her husband, and kidnapped her daughter. Two years later, there is still no information regarding her whereabouts.[10]

There is something dizzying about the seemingly interminable list of attacks and killings, and the sheer repetition and numbers make it difficult to appreciate the human reality of it all. But there is no other way of presenting the truth of the slaughter, nor is it likely that the situation will improve. The Nigerian government is not going to surrender to the Islamists and the Muslim terrorists in turn know that the best way to destabilize the government is to cause strife and even civil war. Christians do sometimes retaliate but never in the form of the regular butchering undertaken by Muslim radicals. And while Boko Haram leads and organizes much of the violence, it is not the sole perpetrator. Muslims from disparate groups and communities in Nigeria, and from elsewhere in Africa, continue to be involved. There is genuine co-existence between Muslims and Christians in some parts of the country but this is becoming less common and under constant threat. Jihadists see their holy war as a long struggle and the aim is less victory in Nigeria than the establishment of a totally Muslim Africa. As a result, there have been brutal attacks in Somalia, Sudan, and elsewhere, and in March 2014, there were killings in Mombassa in Kenya, where sixteen people were murdered in a church, and in Zanzibar in Tanzania in late 2013 when a priest was the victim of an acid attack. Bishop Hyacinth Egbebo, administrator of the Apostolic Vicariate of Bomadi, in Nigeria's Niger Delta, summed up the situation when he said that "if Nigeria falls to Islamic extremists, all of Africa will be at risk." It is precisely what radical Islam wants to hear and precisely what it is trying to achieve. One thing is for certain: many more Christians will die in Africa.

ELSEWHERE

PERSECUTION IS FIERCE in numerous other countries with a sizeable or majority Muslim population. It is rampant in Saudi Arabia, Afghanistan, Mali, Algeria, Tunisia, Turkey, and, frankly, in most of the Muslim world. Saudi Arabia is one of the most authoritarian countries in the world, and apostasy carries the death sentence. In 2012, for example, a Saudi woman became a Christian but managed to escape the country and find refugee status in Sweden. Two people who had helped her, however, were arrested and sentenced to prison. One of them, a Lebanese citizen, was given six years in prison and three hundred lashes, and the other, a Saudi, was given two years in prison and two hundred lashes. The case became a national cause in Saudi Arabia and the woman herself came to world attention and was known as "the girl of Khobar." Although she remained anonymous, she spoke out from exile, criticizing the Saudi approach to religious freedom.

Nina Shea, the director of the Washington-based Hudson Institute's Center for Religious Freedom, helped to defend the woman, explaining at the time, "There is zero tolerance for any non-Muslim religions in Saudi Arabia" but because of Saudi Arabia's oil wealth and its relative support for Western foreign policy, although it may be criticized in Washington and London there is seldom anything of substance done to help defend persecuted Christians in the country. Saudi Arabia is officially Sunni Muslim, its constitution is the Koran, the legal system is sharia, and there is no separation whatsoever of mosque and state. There are no churches for Saudis themselves but Western Christians working in the country are allowed to worship in private homes as long as they keep these meetings private. But their services can be raided at any time by the religious police, the mutawa'ah, who have extensive powers. Bibles, crucifixes, rosaries, and icons are all strictly forbidden, and priests and pastors are forbidden entry into the country if there is any suspicion that they intend to conduct services or minister to Christians. Saudi Arabia also produces and exports large numbers of anti-Christian textbooks for use in schools and colleges and pamphlets for distribution in foreign mosques. A book for Grade 8 children, for example, teaches that "the Swine are the infidels of the communion of Jesus, the Christians." The perpetrators of numerous attacks on Christians in Africa and the Middle East can trace their inspiration and funding back to Saudi Arabia. Very few indigenous Christians are left in Saudi Arabia, and those who do live there have to be extremely careful and clever in how they celebrate their faith if they are to survive. Until Islam developed in the seventh century in Arabia, of course, there was a thriving Christian community and numerous churches; the churches were destroyed, and the Christians were converted, killed, or exiled.[1]

Mali in West Africa is 90 per cent Muslim and around 5 per cent Christian, most of whom are Roman Catholic, while about a third are Protestant. The country was traditionally secular in governance and even culture, and Islam was practised with tolerance and moderation. Since 2012, however, sharia law has been imposed in the north of the country and, as with Nigeria, the persecution of Christians has come about as a direct consequence. The Islamist movement Ansar Dine or "helpers of the religion" or "defenders of the faith" has strong ties to both al-Qaeda and Boko Haram in Nigeria and has taken over much of northern Mali. According to a spokesperson from Barnabas Aid, a group that helps Christians facing persecution, "Horrible crimes have been made against the population: massacres, rape of women, obligation to wear the veil, chasing Christians. All the churches were destroyed in Gao and Timbuktu. All the believers had to flee towards the south, leaving their homes and giving up all their goods." Dr. Patrick Sookhdeo from the same organization says, "Christians in Mali are in a desperate plight. Forced to flee their homes to save their lives amid a violent Islamist takeover that includes the specific targeting of Christians, they are distressed and in great need. The Church in Mali is rallying to help, but in the midst of a grave food crisis, resources are limited and expensive." Up to 300,000 Christians have fled the north for the relative safety of the capital, Bamako, or they have left their country for Burkina Faso and Mauritania.[2]

Bangladesh is an overwhelmingly Muslim nation, and Christians represent only 1 per cent of the country. As in Pakistan, they tend to be poor and lacking in power but they did for many years enjoy a certain freedom and toleration.

This changed after trials of Islamist leaders dating back to the War of Independence in 1971. Demonstrations against the trials by newly emboldened and radicalized Muslim fundamentalists called not only for the trial to stop but also for blasphemy laws to be introduced and for sharia law to be imposed. In the country's 2013 elections, there was widespread anti-Christian violence, even though the Christian vote was so small that it could not possibly influence the result. Even so, churches were burned and Christian villages attacked. In

Bolakipur, a Muslim group smashed its way into the Catholic seminary and attacked the students and rector; according to Corey Bailey from International Christian Concern, "Many Christians didn't go to vote because they were afraid of what was going to happen to them. . . . Christians are spending their days in panic and fear and are never sure who they can trust." After the election and the success of the secular party that opposed Islamic extremism, Asia News reported that Catholics were attacked in Jamalpur. Theophilus Nokrek of the Caritas group reported, "Their houses were set on fire and the assailants promised to return, burn what is left and take the lands of the tribe." In 2014, there were several attacks. In Gaibandha, a young Catholic was murdered for daring to organize a demonstration against anti-Christian violence, and in Jamalpur Catholics were badly beaten by a gang of Islamists.[3]

In 2008, the International Social Survey Program published the results of extensive research by two Turkish academics concerning the condition of modern Turkey. The survey had been financed by the European Union with the purpose of discovering what Turks thought of those around them. The findings did not shock those who know Turkish attitudes toward Christians and Christianity. A third said they wouldn't want a Christian as a neighbour, more than half said that Christians should not be allowed to express their religious opinions in public or in print, and the same number believed that Christians should not be allowed to serve in the army or police or work in the health service. This from what is considered the most secular and Western Islamic country in the world. The renowned historian Bernard Lewis had written, "One may speak of Christian Arabs – but a Christian Turk is an absurdity and a contradiction in terms. Even today [1968], after thirty-five years of the secular republic, a non-Muslim in Turkey may be called a Turkish citizen, but never a Turk."[4] Professor Lewis is correct but, as we have seen earlier, it is also increasingly difficult to be a Christian Arab.

Yet Turkey was at one time the very centre of Eastern Christianity. It was the birthplace of St. Paul, Timothy, and Polycarp, and Antioch was the first place that followers of Jesus were called Christians. For a thousand years, the Hagia Sophia in Constantinople, now Istanbul, was the largest church in the entire world. It is also believed that St. John took the Virgin Mary to what is now Turkey to spend the final days of her life. Today, however, there are perhaps 120,000 Christians left. If many Turks have their way, the number will decrease even further.

In June 2010, Bishop Luigi Padovese, the sixty-two-year-old head of the country's Roman Catholic Church, was stabbed to death at his home by his driver, Murat Altun. The killer then decapitated the bishop and shouted, "I killed the Great Satan. Allahu Akhbar!" He later told the police that he had committed the act as a Muslim who had heard a "command from God." It was a profoundly shocking incident that provoked international condemnation, but that outrage was not replicated by Turkish president Abdullah Gül or Prime Minister Recep Erdoğan, who barely mentioned the crime. It wasn't the first such incident either. In February 2006, a sixty-one-year-old Catholic priest named Fr. Andrea Santoro was shot dead in his church in Trabzon. His assailant shouted "Allahu Akbar" before he killed the priest. In January 2007, Christian journalist Hrant Dink was murdered, and his lawyer, Hakan Karadag, was found hanged three years later, the day following the murder of Bishop Pedovese. In February 2006, a Slovenian Catholic priest was violently attacked by a gang of Muslim teenagers outside his own church, and a few months later, a seventy-four-year-old Christian clergyman was stabbed on the street. In December 2007, another Catholic priest was stabbed as he left mass.

The Eastern Orthodox Church is more established in Turkey, has learned to play more of a political game, and, some would argue, does not speak out sufficiently against Turkey's anti-Christian policies. But in 2009, Bartholomew I, Ecumenical Orthodox patriarch of Constantinople, agreed to be interviewed on the American television show *60 Minutes* and explained boldly that Christians were treated appallingly in Turkey, that the country wanted to see Christianity disappear, and used the word "crucified" when describing the experience of Turkish Christians. Turkish foreign minister Ahmet Davutoğlu was only one of the country's leaders who were visibly angry that Turkey's intolerance should be made public. "We consider the crucifixion metaphor an extremely unfortunate metaphor. In our history, there have never been crucifixions, and there never will be. I couldn't really reconcile this metaphor with his mature personality."

It was a rather curious response from one of the leaders of the country responsible for the attempted genocide of the Armenian Christian people in 1915, when between 1 and 1.5 million Armenian Christians were systematically murdered by the Turkish authorities. It's significant that while most of the victims were Armenian, the killers also targeted Greeks and Assyrians – their Christian faith being the common factor. The methods used to try to eliminate the Armenian Christians from Turkish soil were various and vile: shooting, drowning, burning, strangling, beheading, gassing, drug overdoses, forced marches, extermination camps. Yet not only has the Turkish government never apologized for this hideous crime, it has officially denied it for a century and continues to do so. Others acknowledged and remembered it, and learned from it as well: "Accordingly, I have placed my death-head formation in readiness – for the present only in the East – with orders to them to send to death mercilessly and without compassion, men, women, and children of Polish derivation and language. Only thus shall we gain the living space which we need. Who, after all, speaks to-day of the annihilation of the Armenians?" That, of course, was Adolf Hitler.[5]

Forty years later, in 1955, there was another Turkish anti-Christian pogrom. While not of the extent of the Armenian atrocities, it still demonstrated the intolerance of Europe's Islamic state. The Istanbul riots took place after a false rumour that the Turkish consulate in northern Greece had been destroyed. It hadn't, but for nine hours Turkish mobs attacked Greek Christians. Twelve Greeks were killed, and Armenians and Georgian Christians were also attacked. There were around ten thousand of the latter living in Turkey, almost all of whom emigrated after this. But as recently as 2010, two Turkish Muslim converts to evangelical Protestantism were fined more than $3,000, and this was only after charges of "insulting Turkishness" were finally dropped after a four-year prosecution. Their crime was merely to have changed their religion. Even now the Turkish government is working to take land away from the Syriac Orthodox Monastery of Mor Gabriel, a church that was founded in the fourth century.

Turkey is genuinely powerful and influential, eager to become part of the European Union and also to resurrect its status as an Ottoman-like power. Yet it shows no compromise when it comes to the intolerance of Christians. Shortly before he was murdered, Bishop Padovese had asked the government to allow him to restore the church of St. Paul in Tarsus to its former status as a Catholic church, rather than the museum it had been forced to become by the Turkish authorities. The bishop had given his word that there would be no attempt to evangelize Muslim Turks and that the church would cater only to local Christians and to Christians tourists – this latter bringing in cash and income to the greater Turkish economy. The site was, after all, of enormous historical and religious significance and would certainly be included in pilgrimage itineraries. Even the Archbishop of Cologne, Cardinal Meisner, had asked Prime Minister Erdogan personally to comply with the request. The answer was a firm and determined no.

Then there was the absurd, badly acted, and, to Western eyes, risible movie called *Valley of the Wolves*. Appearing in 2006, it became a mass and massive hit in Turkey but non-Turks find it difficult to take seriously. It shows Jews and especially Christians in Iraq after the fall of Saddam Hussein as conniving, violent, and greedy people intent on harming Islam and stealing Iraq from its Muslim owners. Nasty Christians abound, and the pantomime-style plot leaves no doubt as to the identity of the good and the bad guys. It's particularly odious when one remembers the hellish existence of Iraq's Christians since the demise of Saddam, and how many have been killed and how many have been forced to leave their country. The point, though, is that it led to anti-Christian violence and abuse in Turkey. Christians asked their government leaders to at least distance themselves from *Valley of the Wolves* or show that they did not approve of it or take it seriously. The government reaction was to praise it and, at least in some quarters of the regime, give it a official endorsement.

The Philippines is a radically different example from any other country considered in this book because this country of around 100 million people is 90 per cent Christian – the vast majority being Roman Catholic – and only around 5 per cent Muslim. Yet even here there is violence against Christians. The Moro Islamic Liberation Front, the Moro National Liberation Front, Abu Sayyaf, the Rajah Sulaiman Movement, and Jemaah Islamiyah all operate in the southern Philippines, where the country's Islamic minority lives. They attack churches and shrines, they raid Christian villages, they murder Christians. As early as 2003 in Bukindon, ten homes were destroyed and a Christian was killed; in Cotabato, a Catholic church was attacked in the middle of mass, seriously injuring five people. In Carmen, a truck was stopped by Islamists and the driver and his colleague shot dead. In M'lang, seven Christians were killed and five hurt, one of the dead being a six-year-old child. In Siocon, a Christian village was attacked and twenty-seven people were killed and as many wounded.[6]

In 2004 in Jolo, a teenaged girl was killed and a cigarette seller was gunned down on the street. In Patikulan, an entire Christian family, including children and babies, was murdered, and in Pulunoling, a young Christian couple riding their motor-cycle home from work was shot dead. In Patikul in 2006, a Christian was killed at a carnival; in April 2007 in Parang, seven Christian workers were kidnapped and beheaded; in Basilan, fourteen people sent out to search for an abducted Catholic priest were killed, with most of them being beheaded. A Protestant minister was killed in Koronadal in 2007, and in 2008 in Mindanao, there were extensive attacks: four Christians were dragged from a bus and killed and forty-nine were hacked to death and shot when Islamist mobs smashed their way through three small towns. Also in 2008, in Esperanza a seventeen-year-old taxi driver was killed; in Iligan, three Christians were killed in a bomb explosion; and in Sultan Kudarat, a Christian village was attacked and five people were murdered.

There were four attacks in Basilan in 2009. In the first, two people were killed when a café next to a Catholic cathedral was attacked, a village was attacked, a kidnapped Christian was beheaded, and finally a sixty-one-year-old Christian farmer was abducted and beheaded and his body dumped in a field. There were more attacks in 2009. In Jolo Abu Sayyaf, terrorists captured the principal of a Christian school and cut off his head and then exploded a bomb outside a church. In Maguindanao, a teenaged boy was shot dead, and in Cotabato, six people were killed when a nail bomb was hidden at the doorway to a church. In 2010 in Isabela, Islamists in police uniforms killed nine people and destroyed the village's Catholic church; in Tubigan, thirteen Christians were shot dead – five of the victims were small children. In Sulu, a priest and ten members of his congregation were seriously injured by a bomb attack; in Cotabato, two missionaries were kidnapped and killed; and in Bukidnon, a hand grenade was thrown into a crowded Catholic mass. In Maguindanao, a Christian farmer was shot dead while driving home; in Zamboanga, thirteen people were injured in coordinated attacks; and in Isabela City, two people were killed when a bomb exploded at a Catholic church.

In 2011 in Carmen, a lay church leader and father of thirteen children was beheaded; in Malabang, two Catholics were killed; and in Cabengbeng, five Catholics working in a plantation were killed. In 2012 in Maguindanao, a Catholic village was raided, a woman killed and many injured; in Sumisip, five people were slaughtered; and in Tumahubong, a group of priests was ambushed and hurt. The year 2013 began with a bomb being thrown in a church service in Zamboanga. The next year, 2014, was as bad, even though the army and security services have had repeated success fighting against Islamic terror groups. There is no shortage of Muslims who want to kill and die for their religion.

Scholar and author Raymond Ibrahim makes a very good point when he says, "The one glaring fact that emerges from [2014 World Watch List] is that the overwhelming majority of Christian persecution around the world today is being committed at the hands of Muslims of all races, languages, cultures, and socio-political circumstances: Muslims from among America's allies (Saudi Arabia) and its enemies (Iran); Muslims from economically rich nations (Qatar) and from poor nations (Somalia and Yemen); Muslims from 'Islamic republic' nations (Afghanistan) and from 'moderate' nations (Malaysia and Indonesia); Muslims from nations rescued by America (Kuwait). . . ."[7] He could have added that the percentage of the Muslim population is not a factor either. Whether it is almost totally Islamic Saudi Arabia, largely Islamic Egypt, 40 per cent Islamic Nigeria, or 5 per cent Islamic Philippines, the common theme is anti-Christianity.

In Afghanistan, for example, members of the country's parliament called in July 2013 for converts from Islam to Christianity to be executed, as is specified under sharia law. This in spite of the very small number of Christians in the country and the numerous problems and challenges of Afghanistan. The assembly's speaker asked the Afghan security services to investigate the situation, to find Christians and prevent any further conversions. There are in fact only around twelve hundred Christians in all of Afghanistan, and while almost all are converts or the children of converts, there is no sign of mass conversion or any threat to Afghanistan's Muslim identity. The government has not yet killed any of these converts but they have been arrested, tortured, and imprisoned, and many have abandoned the country because they are terrified of further violence, particularly as Western soldiers leave. There are no churches or Christian schools and the constitution states that "no law can be contrary to the beliefs and provisions of the sacred religion of Islam." Many Christians, of course, gave their lives as American, British, and Canadian soldiers to liberate Afghanistan from tyranny.[8]

At first glance, the Maldives Islands or Republic of the Maldives appears more a paradise than a place of hatred. It's an island nation in the Indian Ocean and Arabian Sea area with fewer than 400,000 people and some of the most beautiful sights on earth. Yet it is also one of the most religiously intolerant countries in the world. Only Muslims can be citizens, and there are no churches allowed. There are very few Christians in the Maldives, and the 0.2 per cent of the population who are followers of Christ has to be extremely secretive about their religion and never show publicly they are Christians. Even Muslim citizens who call for more acceptance of Christians can be arrested or attacked. Tourists who wear crosses may be asked to remove their jewellery and if they refuse can be deported. In 2012, Jathish Biswas, executive director of a Christian ministry called the Way of Life Trust, was arrested at Male Ibrahim Nasir International Airport in the Maldives by customs officers after he was discovered to have eleven Christian books in his bags. The same day, a Maldivian was also arrested for possessing books about Christianity. He was held for twenty-three days and then deported. "While I was not physically harmed, authorities treated me as if I wanted to destroy their nation by bringing in Christian books," he explained. "They stripped me almost naked to see if I was carrying anything else. Customs and police officials would ask me question after question and deny me proper food."

Yemen is a Muslim country of almost 24 million people. Around 1 per cent of Yemenis are Protestant, but there are also some followers of the Ethiopian Orthodox and Russian Orthodox Church, around 4,000 Catholics who are part of the Apostolic Vicariate of Arabia, and also a small number of Anglicans. In 2013, the Open Doors blog, an Internet outreach of persecuted Christians, conducted an interview with a Yemeni Christian, who for obvious reasons was not named. "The body of Christians in Yemen is not very large and there have been several hostile situations against Christians in the past, so indeed believers live with the fear of being discovered or being publicly exposed. Fortunately contact with foreigners is quite well possible for most believers. In these contacts, building a relationship of trust is very important. . . . Over the past few years we have seen and heard reports about both local believers, as well as foreigners being kidnapped or even killed. So honestly I wouldn't say that the situation differs much from one background to another. One difference would be that for-eigners can be deported by the government, as has happened in the past. [Muslim background believers] on the other hand can be 'dealt with' within their own tribe. In that sense, the tension for [Muslim background believers] is very high. Family and extremist groups threaten apostates with death when they do not come back to Islam.

"For foreigners, evangelism is prohibited, but there is some religious freedom granted by the government. However a fundamentalist group would not be impressed by formalities, so if they have suspicion against a foreigner, it can be dealt with in their own way, including killing them."[9]

The situation varies in other Muslim countries. Because of Lebanon's political and religious divide and the size and influence of the Christian population, there is a different dynamic and a different equation. Various civil wars and sectarian conflicts have led to attacks on Christians but this is somewhat different from the experience of Christians in other Muslim-majority countries. The new strength of the Iranian-trained and Iranian-backed Hezbollah in the south of the country, however, had led to a more anti-Christian ideology being fostered in Lebanon and for calls for sharia law. In Jordan, with its British-influenced establishment and royal family, matters are better, but there have still been numerous acts of discrimination and violence toward Christians in the last twenty years in particular. Christian leaders have been taken into custody for questioning by security officers and asked about church members and their activities. But compared to the countries on its borders, Jordan is an example of veritable multiculturalism!

The same cannot be said of the Gaza Strip. Traditionally, Palestinian Muslims and Christians co-existed and even cooperated, and often it was Christians from the Greek Orthodox tradition in particular who helped shape and even dominated and framed the Palestinian nationalist narrative. Islamic fundamentalism has now taken over that role, with Hamas dominating Gaza and being extremely powerful in the West Bank. The role of secular or Christian Palestinians in speaking for the Palestinian people or leading the Palestinian cause is very much a feature of times past and an aspect of Palestinian diaspora nostalgia rather than modern Middle Eastern reality.

Women not wearing Muslim veils, whatever their religion, have been threatened, insulted, and even physically beaten in Gaza. This is especially troubling and confusing for Palestinians raised in the West who have visited Gaza to show support and solidarity. There are only around three thousand Christians in Gaza but they are increasingly isolated and persecuted, and because supporters of Palestine are so reluctant to criticize Hamas and the cause there is little public condemnation. In April 2007, a group calling itself the Swords of Truth in the Land of Ribat attacked two Internet cafés and a store selling Christian books. The same month, the American International School in Gaza City was attacked after being falsely accused of teaching Christian ideas. In June, a Hamas gang vandalized a monastery and a church, and in October, Rami Khadr Ayad, a Christian who worked for the Bible Society, was kidnapped and murdered. In December, the Friends of the Sunnah Bayt al-Maqdis, a group connected to Islamic Jihad, warned that anybody celebrating the Christian New Year would be attacked. In January 2008, a group called Army of the Believers – the al-Qaeda Organization in Palestine – attacked the International School in Beit Lahiya, condemning it for spreading hatred against Islam. Once again, the accusation was entirely unfounded. In February, gunmen from the Army of Islam in the Land of Ribat attacked the YMCA library in Gaza City. In March, a bomb was detonated at the Rahabat al-Wardia school in Gaza City because the school is administered by nuns.

Then there is the Islamic community living in Europe and North America. As strange it might seem, Islamic intolerance of Christians is also manifested in the Western and Christian or post-Christian world by Muslims who have immigrated to these countries. There have, as is common knowledge, been numerous deadly Islamist terrorist attacks in the United States, Britain, Spain, and elsewhere, and while some of the motivation may have been political, it's impossible to expunge the religious from the political where Islam is concerned. If we read the manifestos and motivations behind these attacks, hatred of Christianity is never far from the surface. The Fort Hood massacre in 2009, for example, when Nidal Malik Hasan, a U.S. Army major and psychiatrist, killed thirteen people and injured thirty, was downplayed by the authorities as "workplace violence" or an "act of insanity." But while he killed his mostly Christian comrades, he screamed "Allahu Akbar" and was known as a radicalized Muslim who saw the wars in Iraq and Afghanistan as "crusades" against Islam. In Binghamton, New York, in 2009, a non-Muslim Islamic studies professor was murdered by a Muslim student in revenge for what he said were "persecuted" Muslims. In 2010 in Marquette Park, Illinois, a Muslim convert shot his family to "take them back to Allah," and in Buena Vista, New Jersey, in 2013, a Muslim beheaded two Egyptian Christians. It is surely redundant to mention the Boston Marathon bombings, the British bus and train attacks, and the rest of the long and still unfolding list of Islamist atrocities. All evince a total contempt for Christian values, and in virtually all of these acts of violence, the perpetrators refer to the need for Islam to dominate and conquer Christianity.

In 2006, Pope Benedict delivered a lecture at the University of Regensburg in Germany in which he reiterated a very simple question originally asked by a medieval emperor at the end of the fourteenth century about the nature of Islam. The translation was not perfect but in essence it asked, "Show me just what Mohammad brought that was new and there you will find things only evil and inhuman, such as his command to spread by the sword the faith he preached." It was part of a much larger and longer lecture, and what the emperor, and the Pope, were really arguing was that Islam's monotheism was in fact an already established Jewish and Christian concept, and that most of Mohammad's teachings were already to be found in the Old and New Testaments. Many of Islam's laws though, both men implied, were – a better translation – bad and inhumane.

Within a day there were enormous demonstrations throughout the Muslim world, Christians were killed, and in Europe there were protests and threats and violent attacks. In London, England, Muslims gathered in public places and outside churches to demand that the Pope be killed. They cried, "Death to Christianity" and held banners emblazoned with the words "Behead Those Who Insult Islam." One of the leaders of the protest in Britain told the media, "The Muslims take their religion very seriously and non-Muslims must appreciate that and [they] must also understand that there may be serious consequences if you insult Islam and the prophet. Whoever insults the message of Mohammed is going to be subject to capital punishment." In the end, the Pope apologized for what he had quoted. No apology has been forthcoming from those hundreds of millions of Muslims who believe in the death penalty for those who dare to criticize Islam.[10]

THE FUTURE

SO, WHAT OF THE FUTURE of Christians living in Islamic lands, of Christians living alongside Muslims, and of the relationship between Islam and Christianity? Part of the problem is that in the West, and in a Europe and North America in particular that were formerly strongly Christian, there is an obvious lack of sympathy for and even hostility toward Christianity. In April 2014, the British prime minister suggested in a speech that Britain was still a Christian country and that Christians should be more evangelical about their faith. He was immediately criticized and attacked, even by some of the country's Christian leaders. Such a state of affairs makes it difficult for other Christians to support their co-religionists suffering persecution; they are simply not believed or their complaints are dismissed. If the persecuted were anything other than Christian, many believe, the situation would be radically different and the West would be more aggressive in its exposure and condemnation of Islamic aggression.

Iranian-Canadian writer Marina Nemet, a former prisoner of the Iranian theocratic regime, believes that "part of the problem is that Westerners often see the criticism of Islamic extremism the same as attacking Islam, when the [two] are very different. Using various forms of intimidation, Islamic fundamentalists have done their best to stop dialogue and discussion, and they have largely succeeded. Not all Muslims are the same, exactly as not all Christians are the same. Fundamentalism exists in all religions and ideologies and is not the right interpretation of belief systems but is a mere tool in the hands of power-thirsty individuals who go to any length to control others."[1]

Journalist Raheel Raza believes that while many non-Muslims are confused about what Islam actually believes about Christians, many Muslims are similarly unsure. "The Quran can't be understood without historical context, it's not in chronological order so this gives hate mongers the freedom to pick and choose and while The Quran can be very loving towards Christians as in the following verse: 'You are sure to find that the closest in affection towards the believers are those who say, "We are Christians," for there are among them people devoted to learning and ascetics. These people are not given to arrogance, and when they listen to what has been sent down to the Messenger, you will see their eyes over-flowing with tears because they recognize the truth [in it]. They say, "Our Lord, we believe, so count us amongst the witnesses. Why should we not believe in God and in the truth that has come down to us when we long for our Lord to include us in the company of the righteous?" For saying this, God has rewarded them with Gardens graced with flowing streams, and there they will stay: that is the reward of those who do good.' That's 5:82–85. But remember that the Quran can also create negation because . . . the verse where it says that Jesus Christ is not the son of God is taken by some people to mean that they need to vilify and persecute Christians en masse because they believe in the trinity and that Christ is the son of God."[2]

Be that as it may, in the Muslim world confusion frequently leads to deadly violence, and there are very few Muslim leaders trying to explain the faith in a more gentle and accepting manner. Author Tarek Fatah says, "Of course I think it's really about Islamic extremists exploiting the faith. Most Muslims have very little knowledge of Christianity and they do not associate the Punjabi Christians with the West or Christianity. The Christians suffer because they are poor, considered unclean janitors and [a] source of impurities both physically and spiritually. Pakistani clerics rarely ever condemn Christians in their sermons, not for any love, but out of fear of being singled out when applying for visas to visit [the] UK or USA. The West should do more but it too does not associate with Christians of the East. It's not just Pakistan, but look elsewhere in Nigeria or The Philippines. White guilt makes the West look at Christians in the developing world as a remnant of colonial wrongdoing. But while this might be a misunderstanding of Islam, remember that the Muslim faith in a nutshell is the expression of 'Tawheed,' the unity of God bereft of any associates. The opposite of Tawheed and what is the most serious of sins is 'Shirk,' i.e., associating a human with God. For that reason Christianity with its belief in the Trinity is the exact opposite of Islam and thus its prime rival and one that Muslims have to conquer or subdue. The reason this is not very pronounced in Mosque sermons and Islamist discourse is the fact such expression would be considered hatred against Christians of the West and thus never uttered in public and is reserved for the most private of gatherings. Contrary to conventional wisdom, Judaism is the closest to Islam and the two have no real conflict except for the Isaac vs. Ishmael mixup over the sacrificial lamb being offered to God. While Muslims have no problem with Judaism, they reserve their contempt for Jews. On the other hand Muslims have little problem with Christians, but reserve their contempt for Christianity."[3]

It's a fascinating observation, but one with terrifying consequences. Those who were once Christian are welcome to stay and live in Islamic lands, but they have to abandon their Christianity and Christianity itself has to disappear. Author and broadcaster Farzana Hassan believes that "Islamic history and precedent demonstrate a hostile Islamic response to members of other faith communities. Islamic forces conquered Christian lands of Byzantium in the East and Spain in the West. Local populations were subjugated till such time they chose to convert to Islam to avoid being taxed. The relationship has always been an uncomfortable one. The Koran, which is Islam's canonical text, preaches the subjugation of Christians in Muslim lands at the very best. If they remain compliant as second-class citizens in an Islamic state, they are guaranteed protection of life, liberty and property. However, the result of non-compliance can be very detrimental to Christians and other minorities. What if Christians do not wish to sign a treaty or agree to pay the jizya? Does that mean they are not entitled to these rights which should be deemed inalienable for all citizens regardless of creed? It seems the latter is true in Islamic countries. Boko Haram in Nigeria is reacting to this very prescription and has gone on a killing rampage of Christians with impunity. Coptic Christians have suffered tremendously in countries like Egypt where fundamentalism is rife. The Taliban in Pakistan has been demanding jizya from Sikhs and Christians or else they are [fair] game. The only oasis of tolerance seems to have been pre–civil war Syria where Christian and Muslim Syrians lived with each other in a spirit of trust and friendship. Jizya in my view is extortion, pure and simple.

"Islamic practice has created a hierarchy in society based on belief. That is very problematic for society because citizens do not enjoy equal rights if they do not subscribe to the state religion. They cannot run for the highest office, they do not have recourse to fair treatment under the law, because the law itself discriminates against them. Mainstream Islamic narrative does not uphold universal human rights. I would not say that Islam preaches the outright killing of Christians, however, it formulates an ideological framework in which the second-class status of religious minorities is easily detectable. I have myself exhorted the West [to] do more to alleviate the suffering of Christians in Pakistan. I think it is largely for political reasons that the West is cowering under pressure from the bullies in the Islamic world. The West is not able to preserve its own cherished values like freedom of speech due to rioting and pressure from the Islamic world, how can one expect it to influence policies in Islamic countries? The West, in my view, should take a more pro-active stance in protecting the rights of Christians in Islamic countries. This can be done in the form of sanctions, or boycotts. The West can also open its doors to beleaguered Christian communities of Pakistan and Nigeria. But the West is economically dependent on the Middle East and has strategic interests in many other parts of the Islamic world, which it does not want to jeopardize. The near future looks bleak. The Islamic world will go through a series of convulsions before it can tread the path of progress, prosperity and tolerance. As long as AlQaedah and Taliban types are running the show (and they are in several Islamic lands), Christian minorities will continue to suffer. Anyone who even tries to defend them is targeted. Intolerance toward religious minorities is endemic to the Islamic world. It is inculcated in Muslims from a very early age. The answer seems to lie in better madrassah curricula resulting in a more civilized religious ethos, but that is a long time coming. Islamic countries are governed by sharia provisions, even if sharia is not officially acknowledged as the law of the land. It is very difficult to dislodge sharia once it is established. Anyone seen as challenging it once again stands at risk of being targeted. Islam's religious and political milieu is like a black hole from which there seems to be no escape. I feel that one cannot really talk to people like the Taliban. There is no negotiation with people who have blood on their hands."[4]

Reverend El Shaffie has seen so much persecution of Christians at first-hand that he is less forgiving of the nuances of the Muslim-Christian relationship. As a convert to Christianity from Islam and someone who was arrested, tortured, and exiled for his faith, he is obviously a little tarnished by his experience, but he also lives the Muslim-Christian relationship all the time. He told me in an interview in early 2014 that, "Today there are 200 to 300 million persecuted Christians worldwide. The majority, 70 to 75 per cent, is in Muslim countries, not necessarily just Arab Muslim countries but for example Pakistan and Bangladesh, Indonesia, Iran, and African Muslim countries. The other 25 to 30 per cent is in Communist countries like China, North Korea, Vietnam, and Cuba, as well as India and others. As far as Muslim countries are concerned, in some the persecution is primarily from the state and in others from individuals, but mostly it is a combination. In Egypt, although the law has recently been changed, Christians still can't build churches in practice. In Pakistan the Blasphemy Laws are enforced by the state, while in Saudi Arabia Christians are not permitted to travel to certain areas. Afghanistan does not even recognize the presence of any Christians – they claim the country is 100 per cent Muslim. It exists in brainwashing society through propaganda in the media and schools. It can be seen in forced conversions or rape as punishment, which are typically executed by individuals in the community which could be anyone from acquaintances, neighbours, or co-workers of the victims to complete strangers.

"Of course the West should do more but it doesn't for three main reasons: first, you have the phenomenon of the conflict zone vs. the comfort zone. People think that since it is far from us it's not our problem – they have ignorant attitudes and care only about their own life and immediate benefits. Then there is the issue of economic factors being considered more important than human rights, for which you can look only as far as China and Saudi Arabia for clear examples about how western human rights policy can be affected and compromised by economic considerations. Finally, there is the issue of political correctness and the drive to obtain Muslim votes, which is partly fed by a misguided secular humanist guilt and anti-Christian attitude that says that Christians deserve it. This can be seen in the readiness of the West to speak up on behalf of any other persecuted minority out there, from the Falun Gong to the Dalai Lama and Tibetan Buddhists to the Bahá'ís, but the striking silence [is] about the persecution of Christians who are, nonetheless, by far the single most persecuted group in all the world today. There are a few people who try to bring these issues forward and we appreciate their efforts but it is not nearly enough."[5]

As for the future, he is not hopeful that there will be a profound change in attitudes and experience. "Systematic killing of people for their beliefs, whether in the name of religious extremism or political ideology, will get worse if we don't speak out. We must push our governments to confront these issues in bilateral and international relationships and fora and to use economics as a weapon by connecting their international aid and trade relations to a country's human rights record. We have a very powerful weapon that we take for granted but must not underestimate, which is our vote – we must use it, and use it wisely by not only looking at a candidate's domestic economic and social policies but by voting for governments that demonstrate their commitment to address these issues of international human rights. The future will be very dark if we don't learn from the mistakes of the past, because in that case we are doomed to repeat them again in the future. We remained silent in the past and we saw what happened. And we can't dodge responsibility by saying it's not about us – it's far away, or it's about a different group. It is about real human beings, like you and me, and it will be about us, eventually, so we must speak up now. Our world is a dark place – an unfair place, not because of the people who are doing evil but because of the people who remain silent about it. In the absence of light, darkness prevails."

In the early summer of 2013, an ambassador from Sunni Islam's highest seat of learning, the Al-Azhar University in Cairo, suggested that the then newly appointed Pope, Francis I, should take "a step forward" in the Church's understanding of the Muslim world by stating publicly that Islam is a religion of peace. "The problems that we had were not with the Vatican but with the former pope," he explained. "Now the doors of Al-Azhar are open. Francis is a new pope. We are expecting a step forward from him. If in one of his addresses he were to declare that Islam is a peaceful religion, that Muslims are not looking for war or violence, that would be progress in itself." He was referring to Islam's anger at Pope Benedict after his lecture at the University of Regensburg, even though the Pope had apologized for any offence caused. The ambassador added that the new dialogue would not include the other Abrahamic faith, because we "will not take part in any meeting with Israelis." He didn't seem to realize that not all Jewish people are Israeli and clearly failed to grasp that a genuine religion of peace would surely meet with anyone if it could lead to a cessation of conflict. So far this initiative has not produced any results but even if it did it would surely be one-sided and would not diminish anti-Christian violence and persecution. Christians have, after all, tried to build bridges in the past.

The Roman Catholic Church declared in an official document, "The Church regards with esteem also the Muslims. They adore the one God, living and subsisting in himself; merciful and all-powerful, the Creator of heaven and earth, who has spoken to men; they take pains to submit wholeheartedly to even his inscrutable decrees, just as Abraham, with whom the faith of Islam takes pleasure in linking itself, submitted to God. Though they do not acknowledge Jesus as God, they revere him as a prophet. They also honor Mary, his virgin Mother; at times they even call on her with devotion. In addition, they await the Day of Judgment when God will render their deserts to all those who have been raised up from the dead. Finally, they value the moral life and worship God especially through prayer, almsgiving and fasting." The document also explored the historical relationship between the two religions, admitting that "over the centuries many quarrels and dissensions have arisen between Christians and Muslims. The sacred Council now pleads with all to forget the past and urges that a sincere effort be made to achieve mutual understanding."

This is hardly evidence of a Christian world labouring under anti-Islamic prejudice. Pope John Paul II met with

Muslim leaders several times as he travelled the world and was the first Pope to visit a mosque – the Umayyad mosque in Damascus in May 2001. He even kissed a copy of the Koran, causing some distress to many Christians but clearly determined to reach out to Islam. His successor, Pope Benedict, stated on his visit to Turkey, "This human and spiritual unity in our origins and our destiny impels us to seek a common path as we play our part in the quest for fundamental values so characteristic of the people of our time. As men and women of religion, we are challenged by the widespread longing for justice, development, solidarity, freedom, security, peace, defense of life, protection of the environment and of the resources of the earth. This is because we too, while respecting the legitimate autonomy of temporal affairs, have a specific contribution to offer in the search for proper solutions to these pressing questions. Above all, we can offer a credible response to the question that emerges clearly from today's society, even if it is often brushed aside, the question about the meaning and purpose of life, for each individual and for humanity as a whole. We are called to work together, so as to help society to open itself to the transcendent, giving Almighty God his rightful place. The best way forward is via authentic dialogue between Christians and Muslims, based on truth and inspired by a sincere wish to know one another better, respecting differences and recognizing what we have in common. This will lead to an authentic respect for the responsible choices that each person makes, especially those pertaining to fundamental values and to personal religious convictions."

There is simply no genuine reciprocity. Those Muslim leaders who are brave enough to call for similar dialogue and compromise tend to speak for small and generally fringe

Islamic communities, and they are usually ignored or even condemned by the greater Muslim world when do they speak out in such a way. Beyond words, however, are actions, and the chronic persecution of Christians in the Muslim world, the implementation of sharia law, and the use of blasphemy legislation show that there is no commitment on the part of Islam to reshape its relationship with Christianity. A fundamental difference between the two faiths, and an obstacle to peace between the house of Islam and Christianity, is the differing manners in which each religion perceives its place in greater or secular society. But even this statement has to be qualified, in that Islam does not acknowledge the validity of a secular society in which it should exist in the first place. There is, as we have seen earlier, simply no concept of the separation of mosque and state within orthodox Islam, so that at best the minority religion, including Christianity, can only aspire to toleration and never complete equality. This is totally contrary to the modern Christian notion of church and state, and has been so for centuries. So while even a majority Christian society can welcome Muslims as full and equal citizens, a majority Islamic nation can provide a grudging tolerance in theory, and usually a painful sufferance in reality. This leads to twin solitudes of understanding, or a conversation taking place in two different languages with no convincing or reliable translator.

Islamic scholar and Roman Catholic priest Fr. Samir Khalil Samir believes that "the essential idea is that dialogue with Islam and with other religions cannot be essentially a theological or religious dialogue, except in the broad terms of moral values; it must instead be a dialogue of cultures and civilizations" and of "the totalizing conception of Islamic religion, which is profoundly different from Christianity."

He continues, "In a closed-door seminar held at Castelgandolfo (September 1–2, 2005), the Pope insisted on and stressed this same idea: the profound diversity between Islam and Christianity. On this occasion, he started from a theological point of view, taking into account the Islamic conception of revelation: the Qu'ran 'descended' upon Mohammad; it is not 'inspired' to Mohammad. For this reason, a Muslim does not think himself authorized to interpret the Qu'ran but is tied to this text, which emerged in Arabia in the seventh century. This brings [us] to the same conclusions as before: The absolute nature of the Qu'ran makes dialogue all the more difficult, because there is very little room for interpretation, if at all."[6]

This is extremely well stated. Because beyond interpretation is criticism, even of a respectful kind. Christians may not be happy with criticism, and even less so when it becomes mockery, but for generations have accepted this as a reality of modern, post-Christendom life, and Christianity and Christians confidently expect to face ever greater attacks and insults. Such a notion is completely alien and entirely unacceptable to Islam and Muslims, which is why textual criticism of the Koran is not allowed in the Muslim world, and why Muslims in Europe, Australasia, and North America are trying, to greater or lesser extents, to introduce such ideas of blasphemy into what are generally liberal and permissive cultures. Surprising as it may seem, Christianity is and will continue to be part of that liberal and permissive culture – not in that it defends immoral and irresponsible speech and behaviour, but that as a Christendom that accepts the Enlightenment, it acknowledges individual rights and freedoms, including the right to offend.

Another dividing factor is the tale of two laws. If we take the example of the Catholic Church, canon law is a legal structure designed to organize the governance of Christianity within itself, and Catholic Christianity will employ canon law as it has always been used. Sharia law, on the other hand, is a legal code designed not merely to govern Islam internally but to provide a framework for the relationship of the Muslim toward everybody else in society and also to govern both private and public life, covering most areas of human behaviour. Before becoming Pope Benedict, Cardinal Ratzinger stated that "the Qu'ran is a total religious law, which regulates the whole of political and social life and insists that the whole order of life be Islamic. *Sharia* shapes society from beginning to end. In this sense, it can exploit such freedoms as our constitutions give, but it cannot be its final goal to say: Yes, now we too are a body with rights, now we are present [in society] just like the Catholics and the Protestants. In such a situation, [Islam] would not achieve a status consistent with its inner nature; it would be in alienation from itself [which] could be resolved only through the total Islamization of society. When for example an Islamic finds himself in a Western society, he can benefit from or exploit certain elements, but he can never identify himself with the non-Muslim citizen, because he does not find himself in a Muslim society."[7]

So as much as we might try, and as much as those of us formed in a liberal, Western culture want to see the world as progressing and improving, it is difficult to be optimistic about Christianity and its relationship with Islam. While hundreds of millions of Muslims are offended by an innocuous comment made by a pope about the nature of their faith or by an obscure cartoon in a Danish newspaper, the Islamic world still believes that Christians living in Islamic society are *dhimmis* or second-class people who should pay a special religious tax and are never to be accepted as full citizens or treated with genuine respect and equality. At best they may be tolerated but have to show reverence to Muslims, gain permission to repair and build churches, and must not be allowed to communicate their faith, even inadvertently, to Muslims. While Muslims complain of Christians who broadcast the Gospel into Islamic countries by television and radio, churches are destroyed, Muslim converts to Christianity are persecuted and murdered, and apolitical monks and priests tortured and slaughtered.

A victim and a perpetrator cannot meet in some imaginary middle, a person who is being beaten cannot compromise with the person doing the beating. Christian forgiveness is vital in all this but the new equation has to begin with the cessation by Muslims throughout the world of their hateful campaign against innocent Christians. It is the most hideous, vehement, and widespread persecution of an identifiable minority in modern times, and it is taking place before our eyes. Yet so many people prefer blindness to a clarity of vision that might shock and disturb and shake us from our comfort zone. Pray God for good sight, pray God that the situation will change. The cries of millions of the broken and betrayed scream out throughout the world and for all time.

NOTES

INTRODUCTION

1. Adelaide Mena, "Christians are most persecuted group on earth, legislators told," Catholic News Agency, February 12, 2014.
2. Anthony Browne, "Church of Martyrs," *The Spectator*, March 26, 2005.
3. Hannah Roberts, "Warsi sounds warning over persecution of Christians in Middle East saying it has become a 'global crisis,'" *Daily Mail*, January 22, 2014.
4. John McMannus, "Christians persecuted by Islamists, says Prince Charles," BBC News, December 18, 2013.

CONTEXT

1. *The Qur'an*, translated by M.A.S. Abdel Haleem. Oxford: Oxford University Press, 2008.
2. Ibid.
3. Ibid.
4. Martin Lings, *Muhammad: His Life Based on the Earliest Sources*. Rochester, Vermont: Inner Traditions, 2006.
5. Bat Ye'or, *The Decline of Eastern Christianity Under Islam: From Jihad to Dhimmitude: Seventh–Twentieth Century*. Fairleigh Dickinson University, 1996.
6. Reza Aslan, *No god but God: The Origins, Evolution, and Future of Islam*. New York: Random House, 2011.
7. Jonathan Riley-Smith, *The Crusades: A Short History*. New Haven: Yale University Press, 2005.

SYRIA AND IRAQ

1. *The Arena*, Sun News, March 2014.

2. Father Alexander Lucie-Smith, "Assad's Regime Is Appalling, but I Can't Blame My Christian Friends for Praying that He Wins," CatholicHerald.co.uk, June 20, 2013. http://www.catholicherald. co.uk/commentandblogs/2013/06/20/assads-regime-is-appalling-but-i-cant-blame-my-christian-friends-in-syria-for-praying-that-he-wins/

3. Raymond Ibrahim, *Crucified Again: Exposing Islam's New War on Christians*. Washington, D.C.: Regnery Publishing, 2013.

4. Walied Shoebat and Theodore Shoebat, "Actual and Literal Human Slaughterhouses for Christians Discovered," Shoebat.com, March 17, 2014. http://shoebat.com/2014/03/17/actual-literal-islamic-human-slaughterhouses-christians-discovered/

5. Interview with the author, London, April 2013.

6. Raniah Salloum, Spiegel Online, September 2013. www.spiegel.de

7. Ibid.

8. Colin Freeman, "Iraq's Battle to Save Its Christian Souls: 'Christians Are Finished Here,'" *The Telegraph*, December 15, 2013. http://www.telegraph.co.uk/news/worldnews/middleeast/iraq/10517810/Iraqs-battle-to-save-its-Christian-souls-Christians-are-finished-here.html

9. Ibid.

10. Morgan Lee, "Christians in Syria Will Pay if Assad Is Overthrown, Says Rand Paul," Christian Post, September 2013. http://www.christianpost.com/news/christians-in-syria-will-pay-if-assad-is-overthrown-says-rand-paul-103538/

11. Ibid.

12. James Sturke, "100 Dead in Iraq Bomb Carnage," *Guardian*, February 28, 2005.

13. "Four Southern Baptist Aid Workers Killed in Iraq," Christianity Today, March 1, 2004. http://www.christianitytoday.com/ct/2004/marchweb-only/3-15-21.0.html

14. Mar Louis Raphael I Sako, "Chaldean Patriarch on the Uncertain Future of Eastern Christians, a Bridge Between the West and Islam," AsiaNews.it, March 4, 2014. http://www.asianews.it/

news-en/Chaldean-Patriarch-on-the-uncertain-future-of-eastern-Christians,-a-bridge-between-the-West-and-Islam-30734.html

EGYPT

1. Personal reporting by author.
2. Otto F.A. Meinardus, *Christians in Egypt: Orthodox, Catholic, and Protestant Communities – Past and Present.* Cairo American University in Cairo Press, 2006.
3. CBS News, Clarissa Ward On Line, 2013.
4. Ibid.
5. Kareem Fahim and Liam Stack, "Fatal Bomb Hits a Church in Egypt," *New York Times,* January 1, 2011. http://www.nytimes.com/2011/01/02/world/middleeast/02egypt.html?_r=0
6. Yasmine El Rashidi, "Massacre in Cairo," *New York Review of Books,* October 16, 2011. http://www.nybooks.com/blogs/nyrblog/2011/oct/16/massacre-cairo/
7. Personal correspondence with author.

PAKISTAN

1. Personal correspondence with author.
2. Ibid.
3. "Pakistani Governor Killed in Shooting," B92.net, January 5, 2011. http://www.b92.net/eng/news/world.php?yyyy=2011&mm=01&dd=05&nav_id=71938
4. Personal interview with author.
5. "Sprayed With 25 Bullets: Pakistan's Only Christian Minister Executed by Taliban Gunman After Campaigning for Free Speech," MailOnline, March 2, 2011. http://www.dailymail.co.uk/news/article-1362087/Shahbaz-Bhatti-Pakistans-Christian-minister-killed-Taliban-gunman.html
6. Saima Mohsin and Emma Lacey-Bordeaux, CNN World, 2013.
7. Personal correspondence with author.
8. Personal correspondence with author.
9. Ibid.
10. Ibid.

IRAN

1. Meredith Bennett-Smith, Huffington Post, December 19, 2012.
2. Personal correspondence with author.
3. Liana Aghajanian, "Iran's Oppressed Christians," *New York Times*, March 14, 2014. http://www.nytimes.com/2014/03/15/opinion/irans-oppressed-christians.html?_r=0
4. *Christianity Today*, March 24, 2012
5. Felix Corley, "Obituary: Mehdi Dibaj," *The Independent*, July 7, 1994. http://www.independent.co.uk/news/people/obituary-mehdi-dibaj-1412186.html
6. Mark Ellis, "Iranian Muslim Touched by Jesus in Hospital Room, Later Martyred for His Faith," Godreports, August 9, 2013. http://blog.godreports.com/2013/08/iranian-muslim-touched-by-jesus-in-hospital-room-later-martyred-for-his-faith/

INDONESIA

1. Adrian Vickers, *A History of Modern Indonesia*. New York: Cambridge University Press, 2013.
2. "Muslim Mob Attacks Indonesia Christians," BBC News, April 28, 2002. http://news.bbc.co.uk/2/hi/asia-pacific/1955918.stm
3. Matthew Moore, "Ambon Victims Say Police No Help," *The Age*, April 24, 2001. http://www.theage.com.au/articles/2004/04/27/1082831567391.html?from=storyrhs
4. BBC News, February, 2011.
5. Dan McDougall, "Machete Killings Fuel Indonesia's Religious Hatred," November 20, 2005. http://www.theguardian.com/world/2005/nov/20/indonesia.theobserver
6. "Muslims Storm Protestant School in Jakarta, Scores of Students Injured," Asia News, July 28, 2008. http://www.asianews.it/index.php?l=en&art=12865&geo=5&size=A

AFRICA

1. John Campbell, *Nigeria: Dancing on the Brink*. Lanham, Maryland: Rowman & Littlefield Publishers, 2010.
2. "Nigeria Buries Its Dead," BBC News, November 25, 2002. http://news.bbc.co.uk/2/hi/africa/2510743.stm

3. Aminu Abubakar, "Nigerian Military: Over 100 Girls Abducted from School Are Freed, 8 Still Missing," CNN World, April 16, 2014.

4. Adam Nossiter, "Toll From Religious and Ethnic Violence in Nigeria Rises to 500," *New York Times*, March 8, 2010. http://www.nytimes.com/2010/03/09/world/africa/09nigeria.html?_r=0

5. "Nigerian Military: Over 100 Girls Abducted from School Are Freed, 8 Still Missing."

6. Reuters, "3 Church Attacks and Retaliation Rock Nigeria," *New York Times*, June 17, 2012. http://www.nytimes.com/2012/06/18/world/africa/3-churches-in-northern-nigeria-are-attacked.html

7. Imma Ande, "2 Gunmen Kill at Least 62 in Nigeria, Including in Church," Reuters, January 27, 2014. http://uk.reuters.com/article/2014/01/27/nigeria-violence-idUKL5N0L12AF20140127

8. "Nigeria's Boko Haram 'in Village Massacre,'" BBC News, February 16, 2014. http://www.bbc.com/news/world-africa-26220300

9. "More Than 100 Christians Slain as Herdsmen Burn Homes, Church Buildings in Nigeria," Morning Star News, March 16, 2014. http://morningstarnews.org/2014/03/more-than-100-christians-slain-as-fulani-herdsmen-burn-homes-church-buildings-in-nigeria/

10. "Boko Haram Kidnaps Nearly 200 School Girls in Nigeria; Parents Facing 'Nightmare,'" Christian Association of Nigerian-Americans, April 16, 2014. http://cananusa.org/index.php/campaigns/news/603-boko-haram-kidnaps-nearly-200-school-girls-in-nigeria-parents-facing-nightmare.html

ELSEWHERE

1. Qanta Ahmed, "Persecution of Christians in the Muslim world: We are what we tolerate," *Jerusalem Post*, January 30, 2014.

2. Tunisia Live, April 2014.

3. Julia A. Seymour, World Magazine, January 2014.

4. Bernard Lewis, *The Emergence of Modern Turkey,* 2nd ed. Oxford: Oxford University Press, 1968.

5. William Oddie, "Despite the EU's Demands on Human Rights, Turkey's Persecution of Christians Is Escalating," *Catholic Herald*, July 27, 2011.

6. William Oddie, "The Growing Worldwide Persecution of Christians Shows That Samuel Huntington Was Right: If He Was Wrong, Where Are the Protests from Moderate Muslim Opinion?," *Catholic Herald*, January 23, 2014.

7. Raymond Ibrahim, "The Existential Elephant in the 'Christian Persecution' Room," Middle East Forum, January 17, 2014. http://www.meforum.org/3718/christian-persecution

8. Aidan Clay, Christian News Today, April 2014.

9. "What It Is Like to Be a Christian in Yemen," OpenDoors Blog, March 14, 2013. http://blog.opendoorsusa.org/interview-what-it-is-like-to-be-a-christian-in-yemen/

10. Ian Fisher, "Pope Calls West Divorced from Faith, Adding a Blunt Footnote on Jihad," *New York Times*, September 12, 2006.

THE FUTURE

1. Personal correspondence with author.

2. Ibid.

3. Ibid.

4. Ibid.

5. Personal interview with Rev. El Shafie.

6. Samir Khalil Samir, "When Civilizations Meet: How Joseph Ratzinger Sees Islam," www.chiesa.espressonline.it, no date. http://chiesa.espresso.repubblica.it/articolo/53826?eng=y

7. Ibid.

BIBLIOGRAPHY

Allen, John L. Jr. *The Global War on Christians.* Image, 2013.

Armstrong, Karen. *Islam: A Short History.* Modern Library, 2002.

Boyd-MacMillan, Ronald. *Faith That Endures.* Open Doors, 2006.

Campbell, John. *Nigeria: Dancing on the Brink.* Rowman & Littlefield, 2010.

Cohen, Stephen Philip. *The Idea of Pakistan.* Brookings, 2006.

Corm, Georges. *A History of the Middle East: From Antiquity to the Present Day.* Garnet, 2010.

Esposito, John L. *The Oxford History of Islam.* Oxford, 2000.

Fisk, Robert. *The Great War for Civilisation: The Conquest of the Middle East.* Knopf, 2008.

Haqqani, Husain. *Pakistan.* Brookings, 2005.

Ibrahim, Raymond. *Crucified Again.* Regnery, 2013.

Jenkins, John. *The Lost History of Christianity: The Thousand-Year Golden Age of the Church in the Middle East, Africa, and Asia – and How It Died.* Harper One, 2008.

Kung, Hans. *Islam: Past, Present and Future.* Oneworld, 2007.

Lewis, Bernard. *The Crisis of Islam: Holy War and Unholy Terror.* Random House, 2004.

———. *The End of Modern History in the Middle East.* Hoover, 2011.

———. *Faith and Power: Religion and Politics in the Middle East.* Oxford, 2010.

Mansfield, Peter. *A History of the Middle East,* 4th ed. Penguin, 2010.

Milton-Edwards, Beverley. *Contemporary Politics in the Middle East.* Polity, 2011.

Rahman, Fazlur. *Islam.* University of Chicago, 1979.

Shortt, Rupert. *Christianophobia.* Eerdmans, 2012.

Spencer, Robert. *Arab Winter Comes to America: The Truth About the War We're In.* Regnery, 2014.

———. *Not Peace But a Sword: The Great Chasm Between Christianity and Islam.* Catholic Answers, 2013.

———. *A Religion of Peace?: Why Christianity Is and Islam Isn't.* Regnery, 2007.

Taylor, Jean Gelman. *Indonesia: Peoples and Histories.* Yale, 2004.

ALSO BY BESTSELLING AUTHOR
MICHAEL COREN

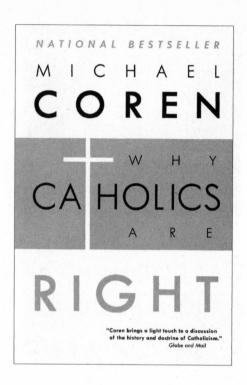

WHY CATHOLICS ARE RIGHT

In this challenging and thought-provoking book, Michael
Coren demolishes often propagated myths about the Church's
beliefs and teachings, and in doing so, opens a window onto
Catholicism, which, he writes, "is as important now as it ever
was and perhaps even more necessary."

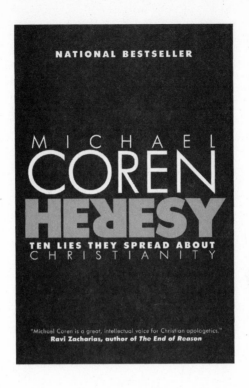

HERESY

Heresy explores why and how Christians and Christian ideas
are caricatured in popular media as well as in sophisticated
society, and addresses ten common lies told about Christianity:
that it supported slavery, is racist, sexist, homophobic, anti-
intellectual, anti-scientific and anti-Semitic, provokes war,
resists progress, and is repressive and irrelevant.

THE FUTURE OF CATHOLICISM

The Church is at a crossroads, but perhaps more significantly and accurately, the Western world is at a crossroads, and how the Church reacts to and deals with this phenomenon will decide and define so very much of the future -- of our future. In this fascinating book, Michael Coren examines the new Vatican -- where it is, where it needs to go, and why it is more relevant than ever.

MICHAEL COREN is the bestselling author of sixteen books, including biographies of G.K. Chesterton, H.G. Wells, Arthur Conan Doyle, J.R.R. Tolkien, and C.S. Lewis. He is the host of the talk show "The Arena" on the SUN News Network. He also writes a syndicated column for ten daily newspapers, and was recently named the columnist of the year by the Catholic Press Association. His book *Why Catholics Are Right* was a national bestseller.